PRAISES FOR *SA*

D0106351

"As someone who is politically active, and involved with urban development, this book is like a playbook for Mayors, City Council, and County Commissioners".
— Topher Morrison, Best Selling Author and
Managing Director of Key Person of Influence

"*Safe City* provides a fact filled insight into community policing. The book highlights the historical police roles and the integration of current and trending technologies which define the efforts of today. The author has broken down many complex facets of policing and technology into a very digestible format. He takes the reader through the etiologies of current, imparting a better understanding of today's efforts and the integration of the past and present. This is a good read that delivers a solid understanding of the "how and why" of the future of community policing in America".
— Retired Deputy Chief Metro Detroit Police Department

Safe City

SAFE CITY

From Law Enforcement to Neighborhood Watches

ROBERT HESSEL

NEW YORK

LONDON • NASHVILLE • MELBOURNE • VANCOUVER

Safe City

From Law Enforcement to Neighborhood Watches

Published in New York, New York, by Morgan James Publishing. Morgan James is a trademark of Morgan James, LLC. www.MorganJamesPublishing.com

The Morgan James Speakers Group can bring authors to your live event. For more information or to book an event visit The Morgan James Speakers Group at www.TheMorganJamesSpeakersGroup.com.

ISBN 9781683506256 paperback
ISBN 9781683506263 eBook
Library of Congress Control Number: 2017945607

Cover Design by:
Rachel Lopez
www.r2cdesign.com

Interior Design by:
Chris Treccani
www.3dogcreative.net

In an effort to support local communities, raise awareness and funds, Morgan James Publishing donates a percentage of all book sales for the life of each book to Habitat for Humanity Peninsula and Greater Williamsburg.

Get involved today! Visit
www.MorganJamesBuilds.com

DEDICATION

My Grandmother—Mary Ellen Hessel

1. Crime prevention - Neighborhood Watches
2. Crime prevention - Neighborhood Law Enforcements
3. Crime Prevention - Citizen participation
4. Law enforcement - Crime prevention
5. Neighborhood Planning - US
6. Crime prevention - US
7. Safe neighborhoods
8. Police - US
9. Vigilance committees - US

364.4
HES

TABLE OF CONTENTS

‖‖

FOREWORD

IIIIIIIIIIIIIIIIIIIIIIIIIIIIIIIIIIIIIIIIIIIIIIIIIII

By Bobby Kipper

One of the greatest challenges facing our communities today is the issue of keeping our citizens safe. Public safety does not happen by accident. It takes a great deal of understanding by all involved to bring about a positive approach to building safer neighborhoods. And this approach cannot be the sole responsibility of law enforcement. After twenty-six years of active law enforcement service, and over three decades of training police officers, it is extremely clear that while citizens want safe communities, there is a lack of understanding on how to achieve that goal.

In *Safe City*, Robert Hessel has done an excellent job of bringing a better understanding to what it takes to build safer communities. From understanding the role of law enforcement to citizen involvement and the use of technology, his writing can serve as a blue print for citizens as well as business and community leaders. While the road to public safety can seem complicated, in *Safe City*, Hessel establishes an understanding of how to navigate the path for all involved.

The current state of affairs in our country makes this a very timely read. From mass shootings to daily cyber breaches, it is time for all of us to look at our individual responsibility to community safety. This is not an issue that we can take lightly. Our ability to build and maintain safe cities will impact our children and grandchildren for years to come. The time is now to roll up our sleeves and focus on becoming a "safe city."

Bobby Kipper
Founder/Executive Director
National Center for Prevention of Community Violence
Best-Selling Author

PROLOGUE

||||||||||||||||||||||||||||||||||||||||||||||

Why is community safety important? Everyone wants to feel safe where they live, work and play. It's a basic human right to feel and be safe in your community. But, it takes a concerted effort to keep a city safe, and there's a lot more to it than you might imagine.

Whether you're dealing with large community gatherings or day-to-day community life, city governments face many challenges when trying to ensure the physical safety of their citizens. Along with handling traditional crime, the growing number of terrorist attacks taking place around the globe should put local law enforcement and other emergency response services on high alert. The need to assure its citizens of adequate protection should put public security at the top of every city official's agenda. Business owners and individual citizens concerned about their own personal safety should become more proactive in helping keep their city safe through partnerships with police personnel and their community policing efforts.

Security measures for public safety have become a prevalent part of American cities and communities. This is especially true following the aftermath of catastrophic events, like the 9/11 terrorist attacks, Oklahoma City bombing, Boston Marathon bombing, Columbine and Sandy Hook school shootings, the Orlando nightclub shooting, and Hurricane Katrina. The safety of any city can be effected by a wide spectrum of potential threats from man-made tragedies to natural disasters, to recurring events, such as serious crimes that have an immediate impact on the community and threaten the quality of life of its citizens.

Many cities' security measures take place behind the scenes, while others are through a collaborative effort between law enforcement and citizens. Public and private buildings and homes, transit points, communication networks and civil and environmental infrastructure systems can all be affected by security concerns. It's hard to imagine everything it takes to keep a city safe, but this book provides much-needed insight and explains how everyone does their part.

What happens in the day-to-day life of a large city police officer? How does this affect the daily life of average citizens and how can community involvement help keep yourself and your community safe? Learn how previous security efforts should evolve with technological advances to enhance public safety city-wide. Delve into the valuable steps homeowners and business owners can take to protect themselves and everything they love. Plus, take a peek at how city governments and emergency response personnel do their part while fighting budget constraints.

Safety begins at home with homeowner safety and security measures to protect your property and the lives of yourself and your family. Do you have adequate security? Are your key vulnerability points up to snuff? Even if you feel you have sufficient home security, are you sure you're using it properly? There's no point in having the latest protection if it's not used for the purposes for which it was designed. When it concerns your family's well-being, do-it-yourself security measures aren't the best, so trust industry experts who're trained to keep you and your home safe. My book also supplies some simple ways you can help prevent crime and keep yourself, your family and your community safe.

Small business owners need security and safety solutions that not only keep their businesses safe but also promote community safety, too. Learn how you can create a good relationship with local law enforcement through community outreach programs to prevent your business from becoming a victim of crime and aid in a secure community. Explore employee training that teaches them how to keep your business safe and implement safety protocols to keep your business and employees safe during all your daily activities. Discover how security technology and surveillance camera systems can greatly enhance your business' safety. Plus, learn the importance of linking your system's audio and video feeds to a centralized, law enforcement surveillance system to further enhance their crime monitoring efforts and how this system benefits the entire city.

Because, in the end, safe cities are smart cities. The integration of effective security solutions via next generation technology has gone beyond a convenience and become a necessity. It allows cities to efficiently address crime detection and prevention, gather intelligence and share vital information between all essential government and emergency response departments. However, incorporating all the elements needed for a cohesive system often involves significant manpower, limited budgets, legality issues and a lack of compatibility between various systems and city departments. Despite these obstacles, compatible, collaborative security solutions that effectively combine each department's resources are becoming mandatory to keep a city safe.

You hear a lot about people committing crimes using technology, but technological advances can also be used to stop crimes, and sometimes, even prevent crimes from happening. Learn about key, behind-the-scenes equipment, software, and platforms that can help identify the criminal, terrorist and other emergency-based activity as it's occurring. My book provides details about unified monitoring and communication systems that provide city governments, police personnel and other emergency response services with the tools needed to more adequately fight and prevent crime, respond quicker and more efficiently to potential threats and promote a safer environment for everyone.

Engaging citizens to help identify possible criminal activities, terrorist threats and infrastructure vulnerabilities through business partnerships garners mutual trust and better police - community relations. From a city official's standpoint, the various technological tools available don't just help enhance law enforcement's capabilities, they also assist fire departments, traffic management, and other public safety officials. City-wide systems become the eyes and ears to what's happening everywhere, all the time. This is something that no amount of manpower could ever accomplish. This can give the right personnel a head start on dealing with emergency situations or the ability to prevent crimes from happening. Thermal imaging and gunshot detection technology are just two of the advanced behind-the-scenes tools used to keep a city safe that you should know more about.

Public safety is everyone's concern. From the highest ranking government officials to the man on the street, keeping cities safe includes the efforts of countless individuals working together for the overall good of the community. Many of these efforts take place behind the scenes with massive amounts of activities the average citizen knows very little, or nothing, about. Community planning and law enforcement endeavors are just two areas where behind-the-scenes safety measures take place. These measures are often assisted by technology that helps track data and watch over a city when budgeting constraints might leave vulnerable areas at risk of heightened criminal activity, civil unrest or other natural or man-made threats.

Community planning isn't just about downtown beautification programs or developing vacant lots, it covers a slew of community development issues that can help deter crime. When abandoned and/or dilapidated buildings are torn down, it's not simply because these structures are eyesores on the cityscape. These areas often attract vermin that could affect public health, harbor vagrants, promote criminal activities and are more vulnerable to fires.

Identifying and developing a plan to eliminate these areas keeps cities safer. There's a direct link between physical environments and the frequency of criminal activity referred to as Crime Prevention Through Environmental Design (CPTED). To stay informed about crime prevention efforts around the city, take an active role in CPTED efforts and future community development and planning.

The planning process works best when city planners and citizens understand how various parts of the community fit together. By delving into the community planning process, you'll better understand the different stages of forming a community plan and the amount of work it takes to keep the city safe.

Besides these efforts, emerging technologies are also fundamentally changing how planning, developing and managing cities take place. By adopting technology tools, citizen engagement in the planning process and communication of planning concepts becomes increasingly easier. This includes publishing zoning codes and comprehensive plans online to keep citizens up to speed and using Geographic Information Systems (GIS) to further enhance public knowledge of community developments.

A large part of law enforcement occurs outside the public eye. Handling 911 calls, writing reports, collecting and analyzing data, processing crime scenes and investigating crimes are just some of the things police personnel handle that most citizens know nothing about.

To educate the public on how much goes on behind the scenes, some cities have opted to hold citizen police academies or public safety open houses. These events are great ways for police departments to show the public all the planning and security efforts they never witness. This allows citizens who rarely have a front-row seat at high-risk situations a sneak peek into what emergency personnel does daily to keep the community safe. You can inspect the equipment needed to efficiently run police and fire departments, ask questions about departmental resources, learn about collaborative safety efforts and interact with personnel you don't see on patrol.

What you won't see are the budgeting issues these departments face every year and how they adapt to budget and manpower cuts to continue protecting and serving the public. Severe budget cutbacks and reduced personnel have forced some police departments to limit responses to burglar alarms, motor vehicle thefts, and non-injury car accidents. Investigations into property crimes, various white collar crimes, and even low-level narcotics cases may decrease with limited budgets. Technology could be the answer for some manpower limitations and positively affect how police and other emergency personnel do their jobs.

You hear a lot about people committing crimes using technology, but you can also use technological advances to stop crimes, and sometimes, even prevent crimes from happening. There's a variety of key, behind-the-scenes equipment, software and platforms that can help identify criminal, terrorist and other emergency-based activity as it's occurring – in real time.

Advanced real-time solutions can include collaborative communication and monitoring networks, such as city-wide surveillance systems, machine-to-machine communication technology and acoustic and optical sensors. These tools assist with detecting crimes and catching criminals. You can further enhance these efforts with technology like high-definition license plate recognition readers and face and voice recognition software. Crime prevention and prediction are also benefited by programs for video analytics and crime mapping software.

From a city official's standpoint, these tools don't just augment law enforcement's capabilities, they also assist fire departments, traffic management, and other public safety officials. City-wide systems become the eyes and ears to what's happening everywhere, all the time. This is something that no amount of manpower could ever accomplish. It gives appropriate personnel a head start on dealing with emergency situations or other problems that might have an immediate impact on the community. Let's look at some of the technology city governments may use to enhance public safety that average citizens may not even be aware are being used in their community.

Cameras play a big role in surveillance, and camera technology has come a long way. While you may be familiar with dash cams and the growing popularity of body cams, city-wide security camera network solutions offer comprehensive, centrally managed video monitoring. Citizens may also notice cameras placed around the city, but not realize that the shift in security technology from analog to digital capabilities allows you to connect to a security framework in real-time. Installing and maintaining a large-scale, networked camera system in large urban areas capable of coordinated command and control centers can present many challenges, some of which include protecting the privacy of the citizens you're trying to keep safe.

Like any large endeavor, budget constraints are typically the biggest obstacle. Small municipalities, and even small-to-medium sized businesses may benefit from lower priced, standalone surveillance options when they don't have the funds for complex network systems. Although these options won't include real-time monitoring or centralized recording capabilities, they still provide footage with access from patrol cars and remote monitoring. As funding becomes available, you can upgrade older systems; even old analog systems benefit from the evolution of hybrid systems that combine existing equipment with new digital technology on a single platform.

However, surveillance isn't just about cameras and the newest camera technology. Advanced surveillance software platforms, network convergence, digital infrastructures and wireless connectivity all play essential roles in everything it takes to keep a city safe. With large city-wide camera systems, the amount of video fed into your central control will increase tremendously and no person could ever monitor this overload.

This is when behind-the-scenes software that aggregates and organizes all your data and easy-to-use platforms to access this data become vital. For example, traffic cams feed massive amounts of data into the system about traffic patterns, which software then processes to help cities keep traffic flowing smoothly, respond quicker to accidents and get traffic moving again more quickly during jams. Once you embark on the mission to install a centralized surveillance system, you'll find a plethora of ancillary technology to further enhance your community safety plan.

Once you have your city-wide surveillance system, you can add acoustic and optical sensors to enhance the video feed. Besides the feeds from government-owned cameras, you should also consider partnerships to also utilize video feeds from businesses and organizations who commonly install security systems, such as schools, hospitals, banks, hotels, high-end stores or businesses in high-crime areas. Installing sensors on city-owned cameras mounted around the municipality can bring a wealth of other data and early warning signals.

One such sensor performs thermal imaging detection, which is invaluable to fire departments in detecting hot spots to prevent fires before they occur. For law enforcement, gunshot detectors let them know when a weapon has been discharged. High-definition license plate recognition readers can detect and read 1,000s of license plates every minute and rapidly check this data against a watch list and automatically alert appropriate personnel when a match is found.

Similarly, facial recognition software identifies people from incoming video feeds, compares them to a watch list and makes appropriate alerts. Besides facial identification, these programs also use analytics to count people, which helps to locate large crowds and generate demographic information based on gender, age, ethnicity, etc. There are even sensors to detect radioactive material. These are just a few of the sensors beneficial to many government officials and emergency personnel.

Plus, behind-the-scenes crime monitoring technology has many other pathways, including crime mapping software. Programs that use Geographic Information Systems (GIS), data collection and analytics programs to gather intelligence and assess areas of the city more vulnerable too criminal and terrorist activities. Having these details can be critical when planning large community gatherings that might attract an act of terrorism. Violence always has more shock value when it occurs in large crowds where the most damage can be done. Mapping technologies also help identify crime "hot spots," which allows police to better focus their investigations and greatly improve crime prevention efforts.

Predicting where crimes are most likely to happen is one of the biggest endeavors that happens behind the scenes that help law enforcement prevent criminal activities before damage to personal property and potential loss of life occurs. Technology helps accomplish this goal in many ways, such as enabling video analytics with machine-to-machine communication. Advanced analytics (information resulting from the systematic analysis of data or statistics) can provide more reliable information to help cities better anticipate threats to public safety, whether it be from criminal events, terrorist activities or natural disasters.

Unlike some techniques, predictive crime analytics study previous threats and the circumstances surrounding these events to identify various underlying risk factors and analyze a broad range of variables. This information could help predict where and when threats might occur, and why. A better understanding of the likelihood of where specific criminal threats might occur, in which areas and at what times, potentially provides a target for police intervention. Thus, reducing crime levels and increasing proactive responses.

Analytics can integrate a wide variety of collected data to compile the information cities need. This can include data feeds; information from public safety systems, such as 911 calls and police dispatch information; and even public sources of information, such as online news and social media networks. After in-depth searches, this technology can provide rapid insights, anomalies, and correlations that could help officials stay ahead of crime. This helps first responders launch a more appropriate, highly coordinated response whenever necessary, which ultimately keeps the city safer for everyone.

However, security for growing cities shouldn't be the sole responsibility of law enforcement and city officials. Public organizations, private businesses, community groups and the general public should all get involved with behind the scenes efforts to play an active role in keeping the community safe.

While terrorist acts have led to heightened security concerns across the country, threats posed by serious crimes and natural and man-made disasters are more common and widespread. Planning for security measures and taking the necessary steps to predict, prevent and deal with any threat should be comprehensive and collaborative. Safety issues affect every individual on both a community and personal level, so implementing a strong security system should be a city-wide effort. Cooperative efforts provide the most effective results and often help overcome the challenge of addressing security concerns while still maintaining and enhancing the integrity of a great community.

City officials can't take a one-size-fits-all approach to their security methods. Instead of throwing unsystematic, partial security measures at problems as they arise, you need a cohesive, practical design of security protocols, equipment and technology to handle both current and future needs. While an overall security system may be a gradual process that takes time, current solutions should be modified to be more comprehensive, concerted and sensitive to an ever-growing set of circumstances that affect the community on a daily basis.

By combining good urban design, sound safety procedures and practices, cooperative security endeavors and modern, security-minded technology, every community member from the mayor to the child playing in the park, can do their part in promoting a healthy, secure city for both current and future generations.

CHAPTER 1

IIIIIIIIIIIIIIIIIIIIIIIIIIIIIIIIIIIIIIIII

Day-to-Day Life

A day-in-the-life of a large city police officer isn't quite as glamorous as it's often portrayed in Hollywood. While the routine duties of a police officer include a large array of tasks, it all takes a great deal of documentation. Even with computerization and technological advances, this entails many hours spent filling out paperwork. Though this may sound mundane, uneventful days can suddenly be punctuated by moments of extreme danger. Few citizens realize the, often stressful, demands put on law enforcement personnel, and the many things police officers do in a typical work week.

Although the basic tasks of a police officer are keeping order and protecting citizens' lives and property, accomplishing these crucial objectives require intense training to perform job functions that average citizens may not fully understand. Police officers are the first defense against criminal activity and they swear an oath to protect and serve the citizens of the community they represent. This means officers play a vital role in peacekeeping through enforcing laws and detecting and preventing crimes. To ensure effective methods are utilized, throughout history, policing systems evolved to meet the ongoing demands of growing cities and the ever-changing threats these cities faced.

Law Enforcement

While some law enforcement duties were once left to the military, according to the National Law Enforcement Museum, America's first known system of law enforcement was established in Boston, more than 350 years ago. Early law enforcement was said to be reactionary, rather than preventative. Thus, an improved law enforcement system was implemented for a more centralized, preemptive police force that was designed to deter crime, instead of just reacting once a crime was committed.

England's development of policing greatly influenced America's development of policing. In 1630, as soon as colonists settled in Boston, local ordinances allowed the appointment of constables. Shortly thereafter, a "watch" was formed, which included one constable, six watchmen, and volunteers who patrolled at night, walking their rounds. The watch members' primary duties were simply to warn of any impending danger.

There is some debate over who exactly established the first state police force in America. Some say the Texas Rangers were first because they were founded in 1823 by Stephen Austin under Mexican law to address Indian raids. However, Texas lawmakers didn't institute a "Corps of Rangers," also known as Texas Rangers, until 1835. This is when official wages were set and they were allowed to elect their own officers. In 1836, as Texas settlers fought for their independence from Mexico, Texas Rangers played a role in the conflict with some coming to the aid of the Alamo; where they fought and died for the cause.

Prior to this, however, in 1833, Philadelphia had created the first-day watch and organized the first 24-hour police force after using the watch system since 1700. The Boston Police Force was established in 1838 and included a night watch and daytime police unit that worked independently of each other. New York City also did something similar in 1844, which became the New York City Police Department in 1845.

These newly forming police departments were headed by police chiefs, appointed to the post by political leaders. Although this new policing method was still flawed, it more closely resembled a modern-day police force. From these early developments, law enforcement continued to evolve, taking on more duties and responsibilities to further strengthen their sworn oath, to protect and serve.

Duties of Modern Law Enforcement

A modern police officer's primary duties always include keeping public order and protecting life and property. Whether they patrol on foot, in a car or on a bicycle or horseback, patrolling officers deal with individuals who break the law. This means protecting the public, preventing criminal activity from occurring, investigating crimes and assisting with apprehending and convicting criminals. Law enforcement has the authority to issue citations for wrongdoing and detain and/or arrest anyone suspected of a crime. They're trained to defend both themselves and any potential victims while keeping the streets safe, even when engaging in a given situation may mean putting their own lives at risk.

Standard responsibilities of law enforcement include public safety, enforcing laws, public relations, alerting proper agencies of safety hazards and serving as first responders for motor vehicle accidents and other emergencies. Individual cases often require appropriate paperwork, which sometimes includes preparing and presenting material for court cases. To advance public service and safety, police officers perform routine patrols and use citizen police academies, school education programs and many other programs to help citizens become more involved in preventing crime in their community.

The more specific duties of an individual police officer greatly depend on the location of where the officer serves. Rural cops tend to deal with lower crime rates and smaller populations, so they usually handle any and all law enforcement tasks that arise in any given day and rarely have the opportunity to specialize in any one area. On the other hand, large city police officers start out assigned to patrol a certain area of the city, called a beat. These patrol or beat officers may take part in a fairly recent policing movement, called "community policing." This concept allows officers to fight crime through trust building efforts with citizens within their patrol area. As these officers rise in the ranks, their duties become more specialized. They're often assigned very specific job duties or may even be assigned to specialized units within the precinct, such as drug-trafficking, murder, fraud, robbery, larceny or rape. Officers within each of these units are specially trained solely to meet the objectives of their given department.

The Importance of Police Beats

A police beat includes both the territory and the time frame that an individual police officer patrols. Assigning a beat is a policing strategy designed to make individual officers more responsible for the needs of the community in a very specific geographical area of a large city. Beats ensure these needs are being met with customized service appropriate to each locality. Patrolling these beats play many important roles. While beats allow officers to better respond, deter and prevent crimes in their assigned areas, they also provide citizens with a sense of security and discourage criminal activity with the routine presence of law enforcement.

It's important for beat officers to foster a close relationship with the citizens within their assigned area. This not only helps strengthen their own effectiveness, it also encourages cooperative efforts between law enforcement and citizens for a safer community. This is referred to as community policing. Although beat police can patrol in a vehicle, they may also patrol on foot or bicycle to have a more intimate interaction between them and community members. Historically speaking, foot patrols are the oldest form of police patrolling and while it's now sometimes considered old-fashioned, it still offers one of the best ways to keep officers in touch with neighborhood activity and enhance community partnerships with businesses and individuals.

Beat officers provide a proactive service that often promotes a feeling of neighborhood safety and reduces an individual's fear of crime. This is especially critical in high-crime areas that may be undergoing revitalization and/or contain underserved populations. Beat patrolling can establish a more personal, relaxed environment where citizens may feel more at ease talking with law enforcement about neighborhood concerns or criminal activity. When officers regularly patrol the same area and engage with community members, they can more easily identify and target problem areas and develop better strategies to solve these problems. This could allow beat officers to reduce the overall crime rate of a given area and potentially reduce the number of calls for service.

Police departments can also combine beat officers' efforts with technological advances like data analysis. This can be used to focus on the times, locations and types of crimes being committed and the results utilized to develop new strategies to further decrease crime. This can provide much-needed data to identify high crime versus low crime areas and determine which areas require heightened patrols. Establishing targeted initiatives through extensive community engagement and a strategic use of resources allows data-driven decision-making that ultimately contributes to decreased crime and a safer city.

While beat patrols still provide a reactive response to incidents, they should also be developed as part of a proactive and integrated strategy of problem-solving. Unfortunately, significant obstacles like dwindling manpower and the increased coverage areas each officer has under his responsibility can undermine the complete purpose of the patrols. This is when a city-wide surveillance system can play an integral role in covering areas where manpower is limited.

Although business owners and residents appreciate an increased police presence in areas troubled by recurring crime and vandalism, low crime areas may not require as much of a presence. A comprehensive camera system with automated alerts can help patrol both areas more thoroughly, but allow officers to focus more on high crime locations. These systems should in no way completely take the place of regular police patrols. Human interaction is still the best opportunity for a better understanding of what goes on in a city, and while technology can substantially improve these efforts, it can't replace the feeling of safety citizens get from the physical presence of uniformed police officers in their community.

Advanced technology also plays a vital role in keeping officers safer while alone on beat patrol. Police radios are an officer's lifeline to assistance in dangerous situations and through technology, they're no longer attached to land-mobile radios (LMR) inside a squad car. Portable radios in law enforcement is one of the most rapidly evolving tools with digital and wireless capabilities that have made communication systems even more valuable. New radios address important issues, such as interoperability problems, and allow officers to share more than just dialog with integrated, wireless Bluetooth technology that can deliver both voice and data over a single communications infrastructure. This same technology provides wireless microphones, but hybrid radios that combine both smartphone and LMR capabilities cover more bases in terms of backup equipment if either system becomes unavailable.

Overall, the best strategy for planning the most comprehensive beat patrol incorporates numerous elements of community policing and technology utilization. Each element should further advance a cooperative effort between police officers and the community as a whole. This should lead to a higher level of trust and stronger relationship between citizens and law enforcement, which includes more, active citizen involvement and a community that not only holds police officers accountable for safety and security, but also each individual community member.

A Day in the Life of an Officer

All this may still not answer your burning question of what happens at the police level throughout a typical day. Although police officers can experience very stressful moments as the first line of defense between criminals and victims, police work is mostly a series of uneventful routines. These include patrolling, investigations and tons of paperwork.

Prior to starting a shift, officers get into uniform and assemble their equipment, checking for any required preventive maintenance or repairs. A shift then begins with roll call, or a briefing session, to get everyone up to speed on what they need to know. Supervisors assign patrol sectors or beats to individual officers and advise them of any special details or assignments they may need to cover during their shift. They'll also brief everyone on any important occurrences during the previous shift, including ongoing crime patterns or BOLOs (Be On the Lookout) for specific people, vehicles or activities.

After a full briefing, officers go to their assigned patrol car and thoroughly inspect it to ensure all regular and special equipment are functioning properly. Officers may replace missing supplies, such as first-aid items, crime scene tape, road flares, etc. Once officers are sure everything is working correctly, fully stocked and stored away, they contact dispatch operators to inform them that they are "in service" and begin their patrols.

When officers aren't assigned to a call, they're generally free to roam within their beat. They will initiate contact wherever they witness a suspicious activity or person. This can include traffic stops for vehicular violations or investigating situations that don't look right for evidence of criminal activity. This may require using his in-car computer to run license plates or search criminal databases for information about suspicious persons. They may also spend time intermingling and talking with business owners and residents about any neighbor concerns. Patrol officers are seldom idle for long as they keep an eye out for any situation that may call for their attention.

While on their patrols, a police dispatcher may notify officers of a call for service in their area. These calls can cover a gambit of issues, including car accidents, domestic arguments, burglaries, attempted robberies, assaults or even just a citizen who wants to file a complaint, ask a question or discuss a concern. Many calls for service require officers to file a report, which they may do in the field or at the police station. Most officers in a patrol car file paperless reports from in-car computers, while foot patrol usually wait until they return to the station. If officers have to return to the station to book evidence, then they may file reports at the same time. Physical evidence of a crime is turned in as soon as possible to protect the "chain of custody," which could be broken, if evidence is damaged or lost when left unattended in an officer's vehicle or carried around on patrol.

During an average day, officers may also have to arrest someone. This could be due to an outstanding warrant or commission of a crime in the officer's presence that warrants an immediate arrest instead of just issuing a ticket or summons to appear in court at a later date.

During an arrest, officers search the suspect for any type of weapon that could hurt them, or illegal narcotics or other contraband the suspect might try to consume or discard prior to being booked into jail. Different cities dictate where prisoners are booked. Large city police departments typically have their own jail, but it's not unusual for prisoners to be booked into the county jail, which is ran by the county sheriff's department. Once an officer turns over his prisoner and completes the paperwork required to relinquish his charge, he's free to return to his patrol. Any arrest requires officers to fill out a detailed report and may require them to testify in court.

Although it's not a daily duty, police officers can also be assigned to patrol large gatherings. This could be at major tourist attractions or during large special events. These events could include indoor or outdoor concerts, sporting events or other community gathering that draw a sizeable crowd. Like policing the city during a regular shift, officers patrol these events to ensure public safety, watch for illegal or suspicious activity and attempt to prevent anything that might pose a threat to attendees. While these events are meant to be fun, there's always the possibility that things will get out hand. A local sports team wins a championship and a sea of people spill onto the court or field, a concert crowd gets pumped up to the point of being unruly or destructive or a peaceable protest turns violent. In these situations, police officers may be forced to use crowd control techniques to protect lives and property. Arrests may be made, if someone breaks a law or becomes a danger in any way.

A "typical" day could also include more extreme situations, such as responding to injury/fatality car crashes or serious crimes with possible threats to life and/or property. No matter what the day brings, whether it's routine or potentially life-threatening, effective communication is a large part of each police officer's job. This includes both speaking and listening, to victims, witnesses and suspects, to unravel truth from fiction. While the public tends to only hear about corrupt or overzealous police officers, there are more than half a million dedicated men and women the public never hear about that perform their jobs with the utmost honesty and integrity. At the end of their watch, these officers return to the station, refuel their cars, turn in any unfiled paperwork and take pride in their role of keeping the city safe. One police department Commander added that, "No matter the situation, realize we are doing everything humanly possible that's within our power to keep you and ourselves safe, because we all want to go home to our families."

Day-to-Day Civilian Life

On the flip side of law enforcement are the citizens they protect and serve. Now that you know more about what police officers do to keep cities safe every day, let's talk about what average citizens can do to help ensure their community is more secure. Because it takes a community to protect a community, preventing crime doesn't just involve keeping your own home secure, it also means looking out for the safety of your neighbors and the community as a whole. Each day, citizens should pay attention to their surroundings and report any suspicious activity they see to local law enforcement immediately.

"See Something, Say Something"

It's easy for citizens to take for granted the routine moments in their day-to-day activities. Whether you're going to work or school, the gas station, grocery store or gym, these routines are what makes it easier to notice when something isn't right in an otherwise normal day. The problem arises when citizens decide not to do anything about it.

The "See Something, Say Something" campaign is a national endeavor from Homeland Security to raise public awareness of the signs of terrorism-related activity, and stresses the importance of reporting suspicious activity to law enforcement. Citizens can take this national concept and use it in their own communities to not only include potential acts of terrorism, but also any other criminal activity. The concept is simple, if you see something that shouldn't be there or witness behavior that seems wrong, then say something about it

For many years, police departments have asked community members to be their "eyes and ears" on the streets, keep alert for criminal activity and report incidents quickly. Prompt and detailed reporting of crimes in progress can get the help you need quicker and reporting suspicious activity may help prevent a violent crime or even a terrorist attack. Once police officers arrive on the scene, they can quickly assess the situation and call for additional support, if needed. Alert community members play a critical role in keeping the city safe.

"You can rest assured that we're doing all we can to keep you safe," said a police department Commander, "but keep your eyes open, because that's where we get our information, from the public. If you see something that's odd, then it's odd. If something in your neighborhood is out of place, it's out of place. Please don't hesitate to call the police department. We will respond if you think someone is doing something nefarious. Remain vigilant and we'll all be safe."

To report irregular or shady activity, as a concerned citizen, you should contact your local law enforcement agency and describe specifically what you saw. Try to provide as much information as possible without putting yourself in any kind of dangerous situation. Include a brief description of the activity you witnessed and detailed physical descriptions of any people or vehicles involved. State the specific date, time and location of the activity and add any information you might have about where the people involved might have gone, if they're no longer in the area. To help you recall the type of information you need to pass along, just remember: who, what, when, where and why. Who did it, what you saw and when, where it happened and why it seemed suspicious to you. Remember, if it's an emergency, dial 9-1-1 immediately.

Suspicious activities that are potentially terroristic in nature may be forwarded to the Nationwide Suspicious Activity Reporting (SAR) Initiative (NSI). This is a behind the scenes collaborative effort to share information on a national level that could help detect, deter or prevent a terrorist attack. It's led by the U.S. Department of Justice (DOJ), along with the Department of Homeland Security and the FBI in partnership with federal, state, local, tribal and territorial law enforcement agencies. This initiative establishes a way to gather, document, analyze and share SAR information nationally, while still protecting the privacy and civil liberties of civilians.

If you're hesitant to report dubious activities due to fear of retribution or concern over accusations of you being racist or any other trepidation you have about providing your personal information, you can always report suspicious activities anonymously. If, however, you'd rather take a more active role with personal involvement in keeping your neighborhood safe, start by getting to know people, then find a community group or crime prevention program to join.

Get to Know Your Neighbors

One of the easiest ways you can help keep your community safer is through engagement. When neighbors know each other, they're more likely to watch out for each other. Get more involved in community activities and get to know the people that live in your area. Attend local social functions, such as block parties or community barbecues, or volunteer for community services projects. If there can't find any of these types of events in your neighborhood, consider organizing or even spearheading one of your own. If you're uncomfortable joining or starting a neighborhood endeavor, at least make an effort to get to know your neighbors. Start with an introduction of yourself or even a simple greeting in passing.

Developing good relationships with your neighbors can be mutually beneficial and could even lead to lasting friendships. Neighbors who watch out for each other's property and personal well-being, help reach the goal of creating a better, safer community for everyone. It's also nice to know that while you're away, whether it's at work or on vacation, a neighbor is keeping an eye on your house for you. A trusted neighbor might even be willing to keep an extra set of your keys for emergencies or if you simply misplace yours. No matter the situation, when you personally know the people next door, you're more likely to watch each other's back.

Keeping an eye on the neighborhood for potential criminal activity doesn't mean you have to be a nosy busybody. You're simply staying alert to suspicious situations, such as an unfamiliar car in a neighbor's driveway while they're away or an unfamiliar person lurking around in a furtive manner. Reporting unusual circumstances has often proven to be a useful crime-stopping tool. If you're comfortable watching out for irregular circumstances, consider getting involved with a local neighborhood watch chapter.

Get to Know Your Elected Officials

When citizens have more access to public officials it broadens their opportunity to express any concerns they may have about crime, safety, infrastructure or other issues. Community members may often feel that elected or appointed government leaders aren't accessible or are unaware of specific neighborhood concerns. This can be especially true in larger cities where government officials have a lot to handle on a daily basis. When there's a breakdown in communication between citizens and city officials, individuals may lose the sense that they have a stake in their community. This makes them less likely to concern themselves with public safety; when many citizens actually prefer being an active participant in improving the overall safety of the city.

Get to know and talk to the public officials in your city. If they're available to hear your concerns, it's up to you to make sure your voice is heard. They may be unaware of certain situations residents are facing. These problems might be overlooked, if you don't address a community-wide issue you feel they could help solve. Take an interest in the role you can play in the community safety decision-making process. You can pose questions, comments, and concerns to city officials in a number of ways.

Attend city meetings, which are publicized in advance. City council meetings are often where you need to request community improvements formally, which should include a list of requests in writing to give council members something tangible to work with. Also, include a detailed description of how each request would better the community in terms of safety. Broaden your participation of reaching out to city officials with office visits or letters to the specific leaders in charge of a particular area of concern. Since one elected official doesn't handle every concern, find out whom you should specifically relay your information. Share any feedback you receive from city officials with community groups you're involved with or any others who have similar concerns.

Get to know Your Local Police

Besides being an extra set of eyes and ears for your neighborhood, extend your duties to include your local police force. Partnerships that join together law enforcement and community members work wonders for solving neighborhood crime and making the streets safer for everyone. Take the time to meet and get to know the police officers who patrol your neighborhood. A large part of the job for beat patrol officers is getting to know the citizens in their patrol area and they take every opportunity to talk with individual citizens in a friendly, open manner.

Ask if your city offers a Citizen Ride Along Program, which allows you to actually ride along with one your neighborhood's beat officers in a marked police car. It's a great way to learn more about the role of a police officer, pass along helpful information about the neighborhood and point out any problem areas you and other community members would like addressed.

Getting to know local officers works hand-in-hand with the concept of community policing. This is a fairly recent movement with the idea that police can fight crime better by building trust between them and community members within their patrol neighborhood. The emphasis is on gathering information and analyzing it to give police departments more accurate information on what's happening in very specific areas within the city. At the very least, community policing often increases the likelihood that citizens will report crimes, which helps get criminals off the streets. Officers simply make themselves more visible and approachable to citizens. You can help promote police-citizen partnerships by speaking openly with patrol officers and reinforcing their desire to familiarize themselves with the people and physical environments in and around their beats.

It's also helpful to learn what crime fighting initiatives the law enforcement officers in your neighborhood are implementing. While conversing with patrol officers, ask about these initiatives and what you can do to help fight crime. You can also add your input on priority problems within your block and other areas along their beats. This helps further build a relationship between cops and civilians and deters crime through a community-wide safety strategy that everyone can take part in. Besides your efforts to get to know all the people working to make the city a safer place, find and join programs that provide active involvement in lowering crime rates in your community.

According to the National Crime Prevention Council, millions of residents fall victim to violent crime each year in the United States. This violence claims not just one, but two victims – the physical victim and the community, which experiences fear and stress over the crime. While the Federal Bureau of Investigations (FBI) states that crime rates in the country have decreased in the past two decades, but to maintain these lower crime rates, it's imperative that citizens continue to do their part in keeping cities safe and secure. The more involved community members get, the more crime detection and prevention occurs. With so many law enforcement agencies forced to cut costs, it's become even more vital for community members to work together to help prevent crime. Local police departments often offer many programs to help citizens truly make a difference.

Neighborhood Watch Programs

Started in 1972, Neighborhood Watch is one of the oldest, and most effective, crime prevention programs in the country. It's also one of the best tools to bring together citizens and law enforcement to deter crime and make cities safer. The program, which is sponsored by the National Sheriff's Association (NSA), took its cues from night watchmen who patrolled the streets of colonial settlements centuries ago. The modern version of the night watch was initially established to involve citizens in a crime prevention program to reduce the rising number of burglaries. Now, it's used to prevent all types of criminal and drug-related activity through a demonstrated presence of a neighborhood watch at all times of the day and night. The program works, because it doesn't rely on altering criminal behavior or motivation, but instead, by reducing the opportunity these criminals have to perpetrate a crime and reporting suspicious activity, so criminals are more likely caught in the act.

A Neighborhood Watch is an organized group of residents within a given neighborhood who watch out for suspicious behavior and report it to the police. While these watches can address a wide variety of crimes, their primary focus still remains on burglaries and property crimes, such as vandalism and larceny. The presence of a watch group can also deter other, potentially violent crimes and dissuade criminals from conducting drug or gang related activities around the neighborhood. It's crucial for

Neighborhood Watch groups to form a strong partnership with local law enforcement. Groups must work closely with police and/or sheriff's departments to establish credibility and receive the information and training necessary to function efficiently and effectively.

Local law enforcement officials can help in every aspect of your watch group, including communication, recruitment, and training. Police can also help you gather facts about crime in your neighborhood through data from their police reports. Overall, a strong relationship with local officers helps ensure your group's success and provides the underlying support for a sustained, broad-based community effort to prevent crime and promote public safety. Contact your local police station to see when you can schedule someone to conduct a Neighborhood Watch meeting to offer tips and training to your members.

Besides linking up with the local police as much as possible, get in touch with a local victims' services office to request training in helping crime victims; ask existing organizations like a housing authority or community development office for current infrastructure information; work with small businesses to clean up littered streets and repair rundown storefronts; and ask local media to publicize your group's recruitment drives and crime prevention success stories. For a more comprehensive program, get everyone in the neighborhood involved from youth to seniors.

Groups should hold regular monthly meetings, so residents can get to know each other and decide which strategies and/ or activities to pursue. Invite your beat patrol officers to attend these meetings, so they can get to know the members and help identify and prioritize criminal problem areas. These officers can also help you analyze any potential problems and develop the appropriate strategies to handle them.

Once your group is established, beat officers may also help recruit new members by letting others know when your meetings are scheduled and provide information about what the group does. You can also recruit new members in many other ways, including canvassing door-to-door. You can also ask neighbors who seldom leave their homes due to medical or personal reasons if they're willing to look out for children and unusual activities in the neighborhood as a "window watcher."

Since watch groups are formed by volunteers, the group's momentum can wane, if your program is too narrowly focused. Try to include activities that fit a variety of talents and provide various roles with respect to the individual comfort levels of your members. Some members may not be comfortable with visible involvement in the group. However, members who aren't comfortable patrolling the neighborhood can help in other ways. This could include cleaning up overgrown lots that may contribute to crime and other beautification projects that not only help the neighborhood look nicer, but can also discourage a criminal element, by eliminating places for them to hide.

Group leaders should always emphasize that Watch groups aren't vigilantes. The members are simply asked to be alert and observant, and never assume the role of a police officer. Always report suspicious activity or crimes immediately to law enforcement officials and never take the law into your own hands.

The Watch system can do even more than deter and catch criminals. Routine patrol groups might find a lost child or pet and get them home, stumble upon an individual in need of medical attention or notice smoke and alert the first department. Neighborhood Watch groups have become so important, they even get their own annual, nation-wide celebration.

National Night Out

Since 1984, National Night Out has been held every August as part of a community-building campaign promoting police-community partnerships and neighborhood solidarity to make communities better, safer places to live. The event is coordinated by the National Association of Town Watch, which was established in 1981. Its goal is to promote the Neighborhood Watch concept and encourage community groups around the country to pool their resources in their crime prevention efforts, which includes sharing crime prevention information with other organizations.

During the event, community members get together for cookouts, block parties, parades, youth activities and crime prevention fairs to demonstrate their desire to live in peaceful neighborhoods. Thousands of communities from around the U.S. and Canada and in military bases worldwide participate in a multitude of local events with the objective to not only have fun, but also document their successful crime prevention strategies and refine their crime prevention campaigns. Overall, National Night Out heightens crime and drug prevention awareness, encourages interaction and collaboration between citizens and law enforcement and generates support and participation in the Neighborhood Watch and other anti-crime programs.

Citizen Patrol Groups

Taking Neighborhood Watch groups one step farther, community members can also join Citizen Patrol Groups. These groups utilize trained volunteers from the community to patrol in marked police cars and provide a uniformed presence in areas where police officers aren't deployed. These patrol groups report suspicious activities and help understaffed police departments patrol residential areas with a greater frequency than would be available, given current manpower issues. Often referred to as Citizens on Patrol or C.O.P.s, these law enforcement volunteers act as the "eyes and ears" of the police department, but do NOT engage in enforcement action. While it's not uncommon for these volunteers to see crimes in progress, they're purpose is to just observe and report to the proper authorities. They aren't allowed to carry guns or other weapons and are discouraged from having any physical contact with suspects. Instead they communicate directly with law enforcement through radios or cellular phones with dedicated phone numbers for this purpose.

C.O.P.s patrol the community on a regular basis, typically in four to eight hour shifts, to perform their primary duty, which is crime deterrence. Although their secondary duties may vary from city to city, common tasks given to members of these groups include conducting traffic control at the scene of a car accident, crime, fire or special event; helping stranded motorists; and performing routine building checks for businesses, vacation checks for homeowners and safety checks on seniors or handicapped individuals who live alone. They may also be asked to investigate non-violent complaints from business owners or residents, which could include gathering information about potential crimes and suspects. By assigning lower priority tasks to these volunteer groups, it frees up officers to focus on more pertinent parts of their job, while also providing a cost savings to police departments.

When implemented property, Citizen Patrol groups become the cornerstone of community policing and help build stronger bonds between law enforcement and citizens. C.O.P.s are known to provide a definitive reduction in a city's crime rate and an increase in community members' sense of security when they see these extra patrols. To help fund Citizen Patrols, business owners who benefit from less crime often donate funds for uniforms, and may also become active patrol members themselves. Anyone with a clean background who's interested in helping lower crime in their community can apply to join one of these groups.

Youth Programs

Citizens are never too young to get involved in helping the community become a safer place to live, work and play. It's important to get kids involved in both planning and carrying out various crime and violence prevention strategies. Youth members can contribute a valuable, new perspective on some of the problems that plague crime-ridden neighborhoods. They can also learn to make positive contributions to their community. To keep youth interested in participating, make sure everyone feels appreciated for their contribution and let them know you consider their role in community safety just as vital as the adults who participate.

Youth-led community service projects that include cleaning up the neighborhood often help reduce drug-related activity. A neighborhood can act as a sanctuary to drug dealers and users when it's dirty or in disrepair. Things like poor lighting, abandoned cars, trash piles in vacant lots and alleys can make better hiding places for criminal activity and streets that permit speeding are convenient for a quick get-away. While youth programs won't be able to tackle all these issues themselves, they can help petition the proper officials to potentially receive assistance.

When residents witness local youth attempting to make the neighborhood safer and less vulnerable to criminals, you can sometimes overcome community apathy and encourage more residents to get involved in safety measures. Funding for the various projects can come from local businesses and government agencies and there are many private and public youth-related agencies willing to supervise eager participants. Residents who observe ongoing neighborhood improvements, may feel an increase in community pride and become more willing to volunteer for projects or monitoring endeavors themselves.

Park Watch

This is a simple strategy in which you enlist park users and/or neighbors to watch over park property. Park Watch volunteers are encouraged to report suspicious or illegal activities via a special phone number provided for this purpose. If cities can't find enough volunteers, they can also ask nearby

Neighborhood Watch groups to adopt the park for periodic checks. Like neighborhoods, signs should be posted stating the park is protected by a Park Watch. The downside to attempting to generate interest in park programs is some parks have been taken over by gangs, drug dealers, sex workers and other criminals, which intimidates people who'd like to participate.

Promote Safer Designs in Public Areas

These projects can be done in a coordinated effort with city officials in charge of community planning and safety protocols and youth-led community projects. The concept is to reduce drug-related and other criminal activity through environmental changes that make neighborhoods less inviting and less susceptible to criminals. Some neighborhoods are perfect hideaways for the drug trade, prostitution rings, and other unsavory criminal activities. As a resident, you can team up with municipal planners, law enforcement, utility companies, traffic engineers and other city agencies to redesign problem areas that make your neighborhood unsafe.

You can help create a safer environment by working together to improve outdoor lighting, building fences, limiting street access to avoid through traffic, installing speed bumps, trimming shrubbery and cleaning up parks or other public areas, removing abandoned vehicles, removing debris and blocking off vacant lots and installing or repairing sidewalks. While it's often difficult to get funding to improve the physical layout and design of individual neighborhoods, patience and planning often pay off. Redesigned areas not only increase safety but also promote neighborhood beautification.

While many people are concerned with potential increases in criminal and terrorist activity, some are unwilling to help provide solutions. Apathy, fear and a lack of civic pride are among the most common reasons why citizens don't get more involved in community safety. High crime neighborhoods where violence is an everyday occurrence contain residents who experience the most fear. These citizens may feel the community's problems are too overwhelming and their contributions will make little difference in the ever-growing crime rate. However, when citizens are vigilant and take appropriate precautions, crime can be prevented.

There are ways to help protect your home and neighborhood from crime. From simple steps like keeping your doors and windows locked or adding a security system to larger undertakings like starting a Neighborhood Watch or Volunteer Citizen Patrol program, you have many options and opportunities to help deter and prevent crime. A solid partnership between civilians and law enforcement in joint community policing strategies remains one of the best tools for crime prevention.

Local agencies who support community efforts in crime prevention can also use various strategies to encourage increased civilian involvement. This includes promoting accomplishments and success stories. This can be accomplished through celebrations to recognize individual neighborhood accomplishments that not only recognizes the neighborhood, but also all the individuals involved. Media coverage and other public recognition is also a great way to show everyone how much they're individual contributions are valued and may galvanize others to join community efforts for a safer city.

CHAPTER 2

||||||||||||||||||||||||||||||||||||||||||

Public Safety
At large Events

Even seemingly tame gatherings and community events can offer their share of mayhem. While small events still require a certain level of security measures, large events require a great deal more advance planning, training, collaboration between various entities and budgeting techniques to ensure public safety throughout the function. When you bring 10s or even 100s of 1,000s of people together for sporting events, concerts, cultural exhibitions, political conventions or other large-scale community gatherings that draw a sizeable crowd, there's always the possibility for an emergency situation. Because, anytime you crowd a large number of people into a confined space, then add heightened exuberance combined with a heavy flow of alcohol and/or other possible intoxicants, you potentially have a recipe for disaster. If the event involves well-known public or political officials, celebrities, sports stars, religious leaders or other VIPs who might attract protesters, or a criminal element, including terrorists, even tighter security measures are required. Major events could require pre-planning as much as 12-18 months in advance of the event to sufficiently cover every contingency that might arise. So, why do cities go to so much trouble to hold events that could be a risky venture from both a safety and financial standpoint?

Large-scale, special events provide cities with numerous valuable benefits. While these benefits can include a significant revenue boost for both the city and various local businesses, well-planned functions can also help enhance a city's revitalization efforts. For residents, special events provide an opportunity for public enjoyment and an increased sense of community among fellow citizens. Along with all these benefits, however, comes an even greater responsibility from local law enforcement agencies to ensure public safety. A critical feature of any event is effective security, which requires police personnel to strike an appropriate balance between ensuring public safety while also protecting community members' civil liberties and supporting a hospitable atmosphere.

A majority of the time, special events, even larger ones, go as planned and present themselves as business as usual for police officers. They'll handle traffic and crowd control and minor incidents of public disorder, public intoxication, disorderly conduct, petty thefts, vandalism and so forth. While most events won't deviate much from typical security issues, some events naturally call for heightened security measures, especially those of a high-profile nature. Large-scale events with an emphasis on political, social, economic or religious themes often have a higher risk of negatively impacting public safety and security. Furthermore, the growing number of terrorist attacks has increased awareness that terrorism can strike anywhere and anytime there's a mass gathering of people, there's potential target, and soft targets are growing in popularity.

This has prompted the United States Department of Homeland Security (DHS) to designate certain events, such as presidential conventions and inaugurations, international summits and large sporting events (Olympics, Super Bowl, World Series, etc.), as National Special Security Events (NSSEs). These events require even more coordination and collaboration between entities, which means adding national agencies to the line-up. Unfortunately, planning for major special events now requires putting almost as much attention on homeland security as it does standard crowd and traffic control issues. This means that joint efforts from multiple federal, state and local law enforcement agencies and public and private sector agencies and organizations is more important than ever.

However, your local law enforcement still takes the lead. Its primary role is the development of a comprehensive security plan, in which it must maintain its everyday policing activities, while also providing thorough safety and security at the event site. This requires cooperation between various government officials, public and private entities, fire and emergency medical services and possibly neighboring cities. Essential details include budget creation, in-depth planning, training of key personnel and necessary logistics.

Budgeting for Security

Whether large or small, every planned special event begins with the money angle. These events can include functions at permanent multi-use or temporary indoor or outdoor venues. Multi-use venues, such as stadiums, arenas, fairgrounds, racetracks, convention centers and amphitheaters, may house various sporting events, large-scale festivals, concerts or conventions, and often provide some of the security personnel and funding. Temporary venues could feature marathons, bicycle races, car or motorcycle rallies, parades, firework displays, seasonal festivals or historical or milestone celebrations, and may be held in various areas, such as city parks, downtown, main thoroughfares or other public spaces, or even borrow multi-use venues, especially fairground facilities. These tend to be one-time or annual events held for charitable causes, specific organizations or community gatherings, and organizers may contribute to the security budget, but typically rely on local law enforcement for personnel.

Not matter who's footing the bill, the security budget for an event is a complete bill of the materials needed to adequately run a security program. This includes people, training, equipment, software and logistic expenses. The funds for a security budget often come from multiple sources.

Funding could be part of federal budgeting, or a federal grant, allocated for security of certain high-profile events, usually NSSEs. Federal funding requires a proficient understanding of proper procedures to ensure costs are fully covered. This includes getting reimbursed for items paid in advance, since funding is often received later than expected. Only functions that meet certain criteria receive federal funding, which can include the size and significance of the event and any anticipated attendance by U.S. officials and/or foreign dignitaries. When an event receives the NSSE designation, besides qualifying for federal funding, the US Secret Service takes over as the lead federal agency in the development and implementation of security operations. For the most part, this funding is either dispensed as part of a Department of Homeland Security (DHS) grant award or appropriated by Congress, but it may not cover all budgeted expenditures.

When large-scale local events don't qualify for federal funding or need additional funding above what's received from federal funds, they require local funding. Most events are at least partially funded by local government entities' and/ or law enforcement agencies' budgets. The financial impact of these events on a police department's budget is a serious consideration. This impact is often minimized with budget adjustments, suitable long-range planning and the support of local government administrators. In light of the positive economic effect these events typically have on a city and the potential for increased name recognition and reputation, local government entities are often willing to contribute. However, a portion of security funding routinely comes directly from the venue and/or organization holding a planned special event, as well.

When law enforcement agencies prepare a security budget, they bring together all the key personnel from every level, including local, state and federal (when appropriate) departments. As a group, they discuss and determine the financial scope of a specific event, including a breakdown of all expected direct and indirect costs. It's crucial that this phase be as accurate and detailed as possible to avoid unexpected expenses, last-minute purchases and purchases that aren't reimbursable. It also helps prepare for city and/or federal audits that could occur after an event. Dedicated personnel are assigned the task of managing this budget, which includes acting as the contact person for all participating agencies. This ensures prompt communication of any issues or changes in the projected budget throughout the planning and execution processes.

Financial management of a security budget is a critical component for adequately covering expenses and establishing transparency and accountability, especially when the event qualifies as an NSSE. Jurisdictions that qualify for government funding for an event must fully understand the requirements for receiving funds and the expectations that must be met. One of the biggest challenges these jurisdictions normally face is financing items they need prior to the event and before they receive their funds. Expenses that a jurisdiction covers prior to the appropriation and/or receipt of their federal funds may not be reimbursable costs. This often leads to the city/agency absorbing unforeseen or unallowable costs it can ill afford.

When a venue is performing part of the security and/or covering part or all of the costs for security measures, their planners may be plagued by financial constraints. With many businesses in a financial crisis, management may feel investing in security is wasted, because there's no "return" on the investment. Further, they may feel that since they've never had issues in the past, their venue isn't at risk. However, with increased incidents of violence and terrorist activities at public events and locales, security managers are pushing their cases for cost-benefit analysis and the importance of being proactive.

Said one Vice President of Guest Services at a sports arena, "We see it as a balance that we always have to strike. There's always a balance of what you want to do versus what's gonna fit within your financial budget. We really try to have the financial budget play a very minor role, and sometimes it's more of a factor than we would want it to be. But in the end, I work for some amazing people that thankfully believe in doing the right thing, including our owner who said, 'I want to have the best guest experience. I don't want it to be focused on the money.' He firmly believes that with the right guest experience, the revenue will follow. Because we don't want to just get people's money once, we want to get their money repeatedly. If someone were to come and have a bad guest experience and maybe not feel safe, he's got the money you want, they're not gonna come back. We want an experience that's going to have people come back time and time again, because they see our building, our venue, our product and our organization as a great use of their discretionary dollars and the entertainment choice for their family."

The need to promote the safety of its patrons' prompts venues to help provide the resources needed for an adequate security budget. Add to this, the various city entities and/or public and private sector organizations willing to absorb some of the costs in exchange for better name recognition and/or who want to provide a positive experience for city residents. However, the number of events grows annually in many cities and the resources required to provide a secure environment and put first responders in a position to better respond to emergencies have increased dramatically since 9/11. Funding security measures can further strain the coffers of law enforcement agencies who're already struggling with sizeable budget cuts and who must limit the effect these events might have on finances.

One of the biggest difficulties in cost management for these events is that costs are split among multiple agencies and departments. This includes expenses for operational logistics. Caring for visiting officers and other security personnel necessary for the event is a large, complicated task. Logistic expenses related to the appropriate care of assisting staff members include food, lodging and transportation. It can also include special equipment needs, facilities for meetings and even safety features like tents for shade during extended outdoor functions. All these items, plus an ample staff to ensure the completion of these tasks, further stretch a security budget and provide one more line item to add to the budget review.

Although large-scale events can involve substantial costs, they also generate substantial revenues to both government entities and private businesses. Plus, they benefit the public as a whole with much needed entertainment and increased civic participation. Besides developing better security budgeting and cost management techniques, agencies also need comprehensive cost recovery efforts among relevant departments and jurisdictions to recoup some of their losses.

Planning Stage

Major-event security planning is a tremendous endeavor that requires collaboration between numerous departments and often nearby jurisdictions. For smaller functions, planning may only require a month or two, but larger events could require 12 to 18 months of pre-planning. During this time the lead agency reaches out to collaborating partners helping secure the event and meets regularly with these partners and other team members while developing detailed security plans and contingency plans to handle every conceivable situation.

This means creating an executive or core team led by an event security director from local law enforcement to identify problem areas and ensure security and contingency plans are comprehensive, consistent and realistic. This team consists of personnel from key participating agencies, such as area police, fire, emergency medical and emergency management agencies. Assignments to subcommittees are made to handle specific tasks, which may comprise people from this team and various city departments, venue or private security staff, local businesses, the event organizing committee and various partners from other jurisdictions.

The executive team for large-scale events, especially NSSEs, start with eight relevant factors to develop their security and contingency plans. These include the size of the event; any possible threats to the event, including any predetermined threats; duration of event; location of event; significance of the event, including any historical, political, religious or symbolic significance; backgrounds of the attendees, such religious, political or cultural history; list of any dignitaries attending; and potential media coverage.

Given this information, the team evaluates and develops a comprehensive threat and risk assessment. This starts with identifying what type(s) of problems or threats might occur during the event. These could include fires or natural disasters, and common crimes, such as vandalism, assault, robbery, etc., as well as, less standard issues, such as violent protests, gang-related problems and terrorism. From here, they develop an impact analysis to gauge the potential damage from each possible threat and determine the likelihood a specific threat might occur. This data is used to establish cost estimates and the appropriate actions needed to prevent various, likely threats. While the main goals are to prevent public harm and damage to property, secondary goals include preventing increased liability due to negligence; loss of revenue for the event, its organizers and the jurisdiction should an incident cause an increase in expenses or preempts the event altogether; and loss of reputation to the event and/or city that causes tourists to not want to return.

Qualified, experienced personnel analyze key areas as part of this comprehensive plan. This includes obtaining threat intelligence from both internal and external sources, which is critical for identifying the problems security details will most likely deal with. To better understand where threats might occur and how to prevent them, they will interview event planners and promoters and develop detailed profiles of all participants. They will physically conduct extensive site surveys and review information, such as site maps, floor plans, evacuation plans, utility layouts, fire inspection reports, aerial photos and more.

Reaching beyond the event venue, they'll also examine the security plans of major hotels participants and attendees might stay and all forms of transportation used for travel, including airports, buses, trains and subways. Some of these areas are a good opportunity to involve citizens and business owners to garner more detailed information.

Whether it's a small or large street fair, a concert in the park or any event that organizers want community members to come out and enjoy and feel safe, local law enforcement and first responders go through extensive preparations to host these events.

"Most departments have entities within the departments that do nothing but plan events," said one Police Commander. "That event is planned, the perimeter is looked at, the ingress and egress is looked at. The walking foot traffic, pedestrian traffic is looked at. The surveillance systems are looked at. You'll have officers in uniform, out of uniform, officers on horses, officers with dogs, officers that are there that you don't know are officers. Everything that can be possibly done from a law enforcement standpoint has been done long before you arrive. It may be just a little fair. You may not be thinking about it. Whether it's one-hundred people or one-hundred thousand people, the planning is the same."

"Clearly on different scales," continued the police commander, "and sometimes other departments get involved and other entities . . . EOD {explosive ordnance disposal}, which is bomb squad, and SWAT teams may or may not be visible. Depending on who is coming, determines how many or what special teams may be involved, the entire team or just four or five members of that team. A couple of departments send entire teams. It depends on who is here. The public can rest assured that before they come on ground, it's been locked down and it's been tested and as safe as it can possibly be."

Planning for the unexpected is the greatest challenge for any event. ". . . who knew someone was going to fly a jumbo jet into some buildings," explained the police commander. "But, now we also have people that think of stuff like that. What if I did that? What if we did this? There are a lot of what if's and you can't bring a pot of pressure cooked chicken anywhere, because you can't bring a pressure cooker anywhere . . . or we'll be on your ass. Certain things you can't do anymore and that's out of our hands. We have to think low-tech, not always high-tech, because Jason Bourne does it. Anything that can be done within our power is done before you come on the ground."

When an event is held at a large venue they may also have its own security staff or hire a private security firm for additional personnel during large public events. They'll also have many of their own protocols and security measures to evaluate and add to local law enforcement's efforts to maintain public safety.

"Anytime we book an event or we share something on the schedule, the moment it's scheduled, we begin to formulate a plan," said the VP of Guest Services, "and that plan . . . considers what level of police support we need, what level of FBI support we might need, and that's police support from not only traffic management, but internal crowd control and use their assets to look at any other investigative things that might be involved with sports in general. If they have some intelligence that indicates a particular artist has some threats or a particular event has some concern, there are assets within their organization vetting all of that, monitoring that, and if they have something of concern they bring it forward, and the FBI meanwhile is doing the same thing on their level."

According to the VP, pre-planning and security evaluations from their own staff might include, "what is the style of search that we're going to do, how many staff are we going to have of our own security staff, as well as, our standard protocol that we're gonna have, how far out is our perimeter going to go, what would be our policy for vehicles coming into that perimeter, what would be our policies for parking any vehicles within a perimeter, what is our policy for checking IDs or checking credentials . . . So traditionally . . . (we) contact the Chief of Police that we lean on, and he's our conduit to police as a whole and they have the ability to bring in any of their assets that they need to. We also have an FBI contact that they do some surveillance and intelligence on any of the events that we have . . . sometimes they choose sometimes we ask to have some of their non-uniformed people out in the crowd, observing, interacting, so that we have additional assets looking at the operation, looking at the crowd, looking at anything that might be going on, so that they can intercede, if we needed to. And obviously they're working alongside with (local) police."

Obviously, during any large-scale event, there exists a potential for violence and clashes between police or security personnel with attendees. This presents a high risk for officer and public safety, which is why local enforcement actively engages in strategic and collaborative planning to not only help prevent threats from occurring, but also maintain their primary goal of protecting the public in a friendly and safe environment that minimizes disruptions and unnecessary arrests.

These goals are why the core security planning team is not only tasked with overall event preparedness, but also overseeing major decision-making both before and during the event. Depending on the nature of a specific event, far-reaching collaboration with a multitude of local, regional and potentially federal entities may be required, and each will have their own roles and responsibilities. Numerous meetings are conducted throughout the planning phase to establish solid relationships with those likely to be called upon during the event. The fully developed security plan should not only cover all the basics, but also be scalable, so it can be altered should information indicate that different resources may be required. Solid partnerships made during the planning phase helps ensure these resources are available should the worst scenarios arise.

Preparing for the Worst

Large-scale security event planning also requires worst-case scenario planning. This means established plans should be flexible and able to accommodate changes in resource demands as the event date draws near and intelligence may indicate differing resources than initially outlined. Worst-case scenarios often deal with natural disasters, sudden severe weather warnings or the effects of ongoing extreme weather conditions like heatwaves. A good example of an emergency contingency plan put into action was when tornado warnings put the brakes on the Daytona 500 in Daytona, Florida in 2014 and the grandstands were cleared of threatened NASCAR fans.

Other common occurrences are medical in nature, such as when attendees start passing out at outdoor concerts or similar events due to exceptionally high temperatures. Planning for worst-case scenarios, however, has shifted to also include extraordinary crimes, especially acts of terrorism that could include risks from everything from hazardous materials to weapons of mass destruction. Even events that don't seem like a probable target, should still have counterterrorism protocols in place to handle any threat.

Even the tiniest details can often make a huge difference in public safety at large events. Preparing for the worst can include something as simple as appropriate trash receptacle placement, which may mean the difference between severe casualties and near misses. The average citizen may not understand the damage that could be caused by a strategically-placed improvised explosive device (IED) or pipe bomb slipped into a trashcan on the sly. Unfortunately, this scenario is becoming a common occurrence. Comprehensive security plans that not only look at the big picture, but also small, often overlooked details like this help eliminate potential threats and/or minimize the damage that could occur should the unthinkable happen. When worst-case scenarios include IEDs or suicide bombers, law enforcement has more than your typical crowd control to deal with and must be fully prepared with appropriate contingency plans and specially trained personnel prepared to respond to the worst scenarios.

"We have specially trained officers and they'll be deployed immediately," explained one police commander. "First, all of us are trained and then there's specially trained officers within the department . . . we'll have an entire squad or mass response team. It takes probably 30 minutes on the long end for the entire team to get there, but someone will be there immediately. That's not counting the SWAT team and bomb squad, who're already there. You'll already have supervisors being placed . . . a command post . . . everything will be there. People {to handle} casualties or injuries will be there."

"We will then call in another department, if necessary," he continued. "We're fortunate in this area, because we have several departments and we all train together, so if we get on a radio, we can say one thing and everyone understands what we're saying. We can all go to one radio frequency and everyone can understand everyone. We're fortunate . . . it doesn't take long for us to be up and running. If something occurs like Orlando {nightclub shooting} . . . people that are off-duty just come in. They don't call their Sergeant. They just come in . . . . If you're really supposed to be working, you're on the street, but the people coming in, answer the phones or whatever. Another department may answer our calls. It just happens. It seems like chaos, but it's an organized chaos and that's what police departments do . . . You just come in. You don't wait for someone to call you to come in."

Collaboration

This is where collaboration can come into play the most, however, collaboration is the key to success in all large-scale event security efforts. Even when a law enforcement agency provides most of the resources, such as for activities in a city park, assistance from other agencies is common. The larger the event, the more extra assistance may be required. This can include other police departments like the county sheriff's office or neighboring city's police departments. Additional key partners almost always include fire and emergency medical services (EMS), but can also include various city offices, such as transportation, public works and the health department, and other public agencies and private sector businesses, as well as, private security and venue security staff. Since many special events are held on private property at multi-use venues, is common for leadership to be shared between the local police force and the venue owner and/or private security. Let's look at the roles some of the different departments play in cohesive, comprehensive collaboration efforts.

Fire and EMS frequently play critical roles in public safety and often have a separate planning team chaired by the fire/EMS services chief. He will either report to, or also be a member of, the core planning team to ensure all plans are integrated with the event's overall security plan. Fire and EMS agencies also have their own specific needs during an event. This can comprise standby and staging areas for various emergency vehicles and clear entry and exit routes for these vehicles. Team members also require clear access to critical infrastructure, such as fire hydrants, sprinkler connections and utility panels. Additionally, hospitals should be integrated into the overall security plan, so vital information is available to primary health care facilities and adequate medical care is available, if needed.

Further up, public health agencies are also often included in planning sessions to assist and advise on the impacts from potential incidents involving hazardous materials (hazmat) or weapons of mass destruction. Additionally, the host city's emergency management director is almost always involved, because they're typically highly knowledgeable about various dangers inherent in major events, such as attendees being crushing in doorways or trampled during intense emergency situations. These directors are regularly responsible for supervising the services offered before, during and after natural or man-made disasters, including weather-related issues and terrorist attacks, so they're also highly useful in developing safety plans that cover these fields.

Many of the facilities involved in major events are privately owned and often have their own security staff or contract with a private firm that handles security on a routine basis. This makes private security members a vital component of large-scale event security and thus, law enforcement agencies also develop partnerships with them. These partners can offer much needed insight into the layout and potential problem areas of the venue and any security issues they've had in the past. Private security personnel sometimes take the lead in security planning, but often, they play a supporting role and local law enforcement takes the lead.

Even higher up the food chain, when federal agencies are also involved in security measures, it's typical for security personnel to work with the FBI, DHS and Bureau of Alcohol, Tobacco, Firearms and Explosives. These agencies bring further knowledge to the table, especially concerning relevant intelligence about any known, potential threats. They also bring added experience in dealing with major special events, since many have worked various events in different venues and cities.

Their presence at the event isn't always a visible role, but are readily available when serious incidents occur.

The lead law enforcement agency cements each agencies' roles and responsibilities with written agreements called a memorandum of understanding (MOU) or memorandum of agreement (MOA). These agreements clarify the legal relationships between collaborating partners in multiple-agency situations. MOUs specify the assisting agencies guarantee on the amount of personnel and equipment they'll provide and outlines any compensation these agencies receive for expenses incurred during the event. It also establishes the leadership of event security forces to avoid confusion and delays when important public safety decisions are required. These straightforward memorandums also give assisting agencies legal authority to enforce the law in the lead agency's jurisdiction, which could be missing in existing mutual-aid agreements that mostly only cover natural disaster emergencies.

To communicate extensive public information to a variety of audiences, an agreement will also be established for media relations. Core planning members appoint a lead coordinator for public information, which may be a public information officer or venue media specialist. Some of the information to be communicated includes general information about the event, such as date, location, event schedule, parking, street closures and so on. Other vital information will cover safety, which includes data like a list of items allowed and not allowed at the event, emergency evacuation information, pre-entry searches, signs of possible terrorist activity, etc. Any information provided to the public must be consistent and developing a handbook containing important public information for officers working the event is always helpful.

In larger cities where events are commonly held at the same facility, it's beneficial for the venue to develop long-standing relationships with the those involved in the security process. It's also prudent for the same individuals from the various participating agencies to become a permanent part of this process. This helps ensure each person on the security team is completely familiar with the facility and the other members involved. The mitigates the need for new personnel to learn and understand important safety factors of a specific venue, such as crowd flow, evacuation routes, security checkpoints and various built-in security features and technology. It may also minimize costs for training to get up to speed on these factors.

Training

Many law enforcement agencies often wish they'd received more training prior to an event, especially when working with personnel from outside agencies they aren't used to working with. It's critical that everyone involved in the safety and security plan is fully briefed on the agencies' expectations, standards and professionalism expected of each of them. Briefs are important part of the training process, because it provides vital information, such as scheduled shifts, transportation routes, communication protocols, credentialing procedures, logistics, details of the overall operational security plan and information about any important event participant(s) that may require extra protection. While training should focus on non-confrontational team policing, specific training approaches are varied, but many agencies have found several beneficial in their endeavors.

Some exercises, such as tabletop exercises, not only involve law enforcement agencies, but also other key security personnel. These can include partners from fire, EMS and health departments, hospitals, private security personnel, other government officials and, in some cases, private bodyguards. Live training events that stage a variety of terrorist attacks and other man-made and natural disasters are beneficial to police, fire, EMS and other day-of-event security personnel. Police personnel may also gain further insight from special classes dedicated to a specific event that teaches about venue security, team operation procedures, surveillance techniques, proper use of riot gear, etc. Classes may be expanded to include training in specialized areas, such crowd control tactics for events in which protesters are expected to become unruly or proper use of hazmat or other protective equipment. Training doesn't have to stop once the event begins, especially if the event lasts several days. Training during an event helps keep officers focused on what could happen and maintains continued attention to pertinent details. Overall, training should be a joint effort between all participating agencies to ensure fluid results.

"There is often joint training," said the police commander, "so not just {the} police department . . . fire departments, first responders, all train together, so they're all on the same page for stuff like this. My department {is also} involved in a regional situation, so our bomb squads are regional and they train with everyone in this region. Our SWAT teams train with all the SWAT teams in the region. They also include first responders from the fire department. Our mass incident response teams will all train together. If something happens that's enormous, you can have an officer from any municipality, any Sherriff's department in this part of the state can come and follow one verbal command and everyone will understand it. Any commander can take charge and everyone will understand."

If a jurisdiction routinely handles special events at the same venue, it's also beneficial to train regularly at this facility. Event security training can be built around both basic and in-service training.

"We encourage all the local law enforcement to use our building as a training facility," said the VP of Guest Services. "So, at different times, they will do drills in our building or . . . they'll bring their dogs in and it will be a phase. We've had them do some SWAT things in the building {and} they've done some active shooter drills. Our purpose for offering the building is, one, we want to be an asset to public service and entities within the area, but there's also the kind of backhand asset to us . . . . {the} more of them that are familiar with our building and familiar with us, the better their response is going to be should there be something bad. As I always say to these guys, 'No. I want to get to know you well before we have an emergency cause in an emergency, well it's not the time to get to know somebody.'"

"We try to engage with them," continued the VP, "and get those guys to utilize our building and we meet with them on a regular basis. Are we training alongside with them? Not necessarily. They tend to do their training, we do ours. There are intentionally times when we bring {them} in. If we're going to train some of our staff on explosives or what to look for in a suspicious package, we've brought in the FBI and let them bring all their suspicious things, then they spread them out and they talk through with our staff . . . you see a lot of really wide eyes. We've also brought in {local} police to do trainings for us on active shooters with our staff. So, it's more we bring in some of their assets to help train our staff and they do the job of keeping us up to speed on that."

Security During the Event

After the budget's set, the security plan in place, training complete and collaborations formed, it's time for the big day. Appropriate security and public safety during the event is what it all the detailed planning comes down to. It begins with a final briefing to pass along key points and any last-minute changes, which are held several hours prior to the start of the event. It's beneficial to brief all personnel involved at the same time when possible. However, if an event is scheduled over several days and/ or during multiple shifts, then additional briefings are held at the beginning of each day and/or shift change. There are many items typically covered in these briefings, but some included items are last-minute intelligence reports, specific assignments, logistics plans, communications or radio protocol and rules of engagement.

Following this, the next phase begins right before attendees and/or participants arrive at the event site. Tasks performed should ensure key operations are functioning properly, including the communications command center, access control points and credentialing stations (where people who gained special access privileges, following a background check performed prior to the event, picks up their special badges). Pre-event checks also involve surveying the overall readiness of the venue and various support areas, such as intelligence and arrest processing, EMS and fire department zones and mobile field forces in charge of crowd control.

Besides a fully prepared security staff, day-of security operations likely include security video and access controls, like checkpoints and, sometimes, pre-entry searches or "pat-downs." Each are important measures for helping ensure public safety.

Increasing situational awareness is often obtained through surveillance or security video. This could come from security cameras placed throughout the venue with data feeds linked to monitors in a security room. These feeds shouldn't just be recorded; personnel should also be on hand to observe real-time videos to look for suspicious activity to report to ground troops. Besides these security video feeds, officers should also be equipped with wearable body cameras to add to security awareness.

Access controls or checkpoints provide a secure entrance point for attendees. A properly managed checkpoint helps ensure threats are detected prior to impacting other attendees. When these access controls are poorly managed, however, they can lead to long lines, angry attendees and lost revenue for the event. Checkpoints sometimes utilize magnetometers (full-body walk-through x-ray machines) or metal detector wands and sometimes full pat-downs.

Pre-entry searches are sometimes part of the access controls of an event and often face legal challenges. Mandatory pat-downs are increasingly viewed as illegal search and seizures. To sidestep this issue, some venues have make pat-downs a condition of entry. In other words, if an attendee doesn't want to voluntarily submit to the search, then they can't enter the venue. This often avoids a potential constitutional clash.

Once attendees are inside, security personnel have a laundry list of issues that might arise. Crowd control can become a key disturbance depending on the nature of the event and the extent to which protesters of the event might cause a legitimate threat or the likelihood of a celebratory free-for-all.

While most crowd control issues can be managed with a soft approach, other events with obvious protest movements and a history of extremist groups causing a major fracas, require law enforcement to have a substantial, fully trained riot control unit ready for a mass arrest situation. Other crowd control challenges can include handling lost children, enforcing juvenile curfews, prohibiting alcohol and enforcing alcohol violations, managing gang-related crimes and enforcing official rules for ejection from an event.

Technology Helps Get the Job Done

Soft targets are becoming increasingly popular for terrorist attacks. Improved security systems and advanced technology, such as bomb detectors and alarm devices, not only assist security measures at large events, it's also beneficial to other places where large groups regularly congregate. Hardening potential targets against terrorism helps protect any place from the threat of an attack. While these and other threats during large-scale special events will never be fully eliminated, there many things law enforcement and security personnel can do to minimize risks without overwhelming attendees. As these threats continue to evolve, so does modern technology. This continued technological growth helps event security stay ahead of threats, while helping maintain an environment the public desires, and expects.

To help utilize this technology, adding crime and intelligence analysts to your security support staff for large events is highly effective and should be brought on board from the outset. These analysts ensure the hardware, software and data for various incidents are prepared and updated on a regular basis. They can also help by creating and updating visual map templates for specific events. Additionally, their maintenance and continual updates of hardware and software helps avoid the use of new technology during an event. By using and enhancing proven technologies during an event, security personnel reduce unforeseen technical challenges from arising.

Communication technology plays a major role and radio interoperability is vital to reliable communication between all participating agencies. Advanced communications technology links radios with different frequencies into a common communications matrix, which allows personnel from multiple agencies using different radio models and frequencies to communicate in the field. This matrix acts as a networking gateway to interconnect any radio with any frequency into one common frequency. To ensure everything is operational and working properly, all radios should be checked or "pinged" in the field prior to activities beginning on the day of the event.

Other evolving technologies that might be useful include wireless voice and data transmissions and encrypting capabilities for radio transmissions. However, one of the most important components for major event security is an integrated communications command center, which can include voice and video feeds. It's essential to have effective radio communications between field personnel and the central communications command post throughout an event, so this technology should be well tested prior to implementing a security plan.

Post Event Review

Once an event ends and the crowd has dispersed, the security team has a few final responsibilities. These include returning equipment and inventory, removing temporary barriers and barricades, paying/issuing bills and completing final administration and logistics plans. To learn more effective techniques for future events, a post-event review or after-action report is a highly valuable tool and should be part of any debriefings. These debriefings should include interviews and surveys of all supervisors from local and assisting law enforcement agencies and participating partners from other departments.

A comprehensive post-event review that includes perceived successes, new lessons learned and details on areas that need improved security measures help the planning phase of future events. Besides debriefings, you can also gather critical information through critiques of various operations, especially your access points and communications personnel. For multiple-day events, ask supervisors to write daily critiques to submit at the end of the event, so important details aren't forgotten. Take special note of any deviations made from the original event security plan and why these deviations occurred. Ask for recommendations from key personnel on what should be kept or changed in future security plans and why.

The Bottom Line

Maintaining a safe, secure environment during large public events is accomplished through carefully planned security operations and successful collaborations between multiple agencies before, during and after each event. The overall key, however, is balancing effective security solutions, while not ruining attendee experience. While it's naive of event guests to not expect some sort of security measures, they're still only willing to tolerate so much. However, efficient security that makes patrons feel safe, doesn't have to be inconvenient.

"The core foundation is an overall view of safety and security," said the VP of Guest Services, "it's an essential part of our guest experience. We believe that there's no way you can have a good guest experience if people don't feel safe. So, on any given day or any given event, we are always putting in play an appropriate plan to provide the proper guest experience and the proper security plan."

"We try to see the experience and security as a bit of a balancing {act}, continued the VP, "because, you know, public opinion, they want to be safe, but they don't want to be inconvenienced. So, we try to balance . . . the right things that make the experience safe, but also not so cumbersome and intrusive that it's too inconvenient and will make people start {saying}, 'securities too hard, I don't wanna go to that event.' But, if you did the reverse, you didn't do enough and it made it too easy is that sending a message not only to your fans that it's not as safe . . . or to someone that may be looking at you as target {thinking}, 'oh that's an easy place they might choose to be a target for some nefarious act.'"

In the end, each venue, event organizer or security planner must consider all the security measures that could conceivably be taken and weigh them against their desire to create an event that patrons find enjoyable and will be well attended and profitable.

CHAPTER 3

||||||||||||||||||||||||||||||||||||||||||||||

Home Safe and Sound

Although burglary is one of the easiest crimes to prevent, it's also one of the most common threats to homeowners (and renters) around the country. Like many homeowners, you may not even realize all the little things that make your home more vulnerable to intruders and property crime. While some burglaries are a crime of opportunity, many burglaries aren't as random as they seem. Many intruders often use a selection process. When choosing a target, they look for unoccupied homes and narrow their choices based on which ones have the easiest access, most available hiding places and best escape routes. A good criminal can burglarize your home in less than 10 minutes. As a homeowner, your job is to make their criminal activity as risky and difficult as possible. Some of the best defenses are those that impede intruders from getting inside at all.

According to the FBI's Criminal Justice Information Services Division, there are more than two million burglaries reported every year in the U.S. In 2013, the nation saw more than 5,400 burglaries reported every day, which adds up to one burglary about every 16 seconds. When your home becomes part of this statistic, you don't just lose your valuables, you feel violated and lose your sense of safety and security.

Coming home to discover a break-in is frightening enough, but this trauma is even more intense for those who are home during the crime. According to a survey conducted by the U.S. Department of Justice (DOJ), a member of the household is home in nearly three out of every 10 burglaries and 7% of these people experience some type of violence during the event. Burglaries are inherently a non-confrontational property crime. However, unexpected persons discovered inside the house or unsuspecting people returning home during the crime can turn a B & E (breaking and entering) into a violent standoff when the burglar flees to avoid being caught. Worse still are home invasions when intruders intentionally enter an occupied house with not only robbery, but also physical violence, the intended purpose.

If you don't want you or your home to become a statistic, deter intruders by "hardening" the target to make your residence less vulnerable. Professional burglars may "case" homes for several days and research individual homeowners or entire neighborhoods prior to choosing likely targets. Research shows that burglars generally bypass houses that require too much effort, time and/or noise to gain access. Experienced burglars look for easy targets, because their goal is to quickly break in, grab expensive items they can easily convert to cash and escape unnoticed. If it takes more than a few minutes to break-in, burglars often abandon their intended target for an easier one.

Strengthening your home's defenses helps prevent it from being an easy mark. You can accomplish this in a number of ways. Start by keeping all your windows and doors closed and locked and installing high-quality doors and locks. You can eliminate hiding places and blind spots by clearing up problem areas in your landscaping and strategically placing lights and motion detectors around dark or shadowed areas. Create multiple layers of defense to make it as difficult as possible for thieves to gain access to your home. Investing in a home security system further thwarts a burglar's efforts and alerts someone should he finally make it inside. The most effective burglar alarms not only sound off inside the home, but also ring to an outside monitoring service. These are just some of the ways you can boost your home's security and make it more burglary-resistant. Doing a home security assessment is invaluable in determining where you might have vulnerable points that need addressing.

Vulnerability Assessment

Pretend you're a burglar. Actually "case" your own home, like a burglar would, and look for the easiest entrance points. If it helps, think about how you would get in, if you were locked out and there wasn't a spare key. Even when a house is locked up tight and you think you've made it impenetrable, there are still many ways it may remain vulnerable. An effective residential security strategy starts from the outside and works its way indoors.

Your security strategy is only as good as the weakest link, such as a locked door with a spare key left in an obvious, easily accessible location like under the doormat or nearby flower pot or atop the door seal. These are the first places an intruder looks. It's much safer to leave a spare with a trusted friend or neighbor. Where do you keep your spare keys and how strong are the locks those keys go to?

High-quality locks when installed and used correctly should be a crucial element of your vulnerability assessment. If you can impede burglars from getting inside, your contents remain safe. Your burglary prevention strategy should include an in-depth look at every single lock securing your home and any outbuildings you might have. Then, move on to inspecting the quality and safety of each door and window.

Speaking of locks and doors, let's look at some human error vulnerabilities you should make sure aren't happening in your home. While locking up before you leave seems like a given, according to a 2010 report by the DOJ, almost 40% of burglars enter through an unlocked door or window. A lock is useless when it's not engaged. This could be an even larger factor in warmer months when you might open windows and forget to close them when you go out. An open window in a vacant home is like a neon "Welcome" sign to criminals. Another 17% of burglars gain access through a door or window that wasn't just left unlocked, but wide open. This means, almost half of the burglaries in this study occurred because a window or door was left unlocked and/or open, which makes human error a top security concern.

Your vulnerability assessment should also include contemplating whether to install a new alarm system or upgrade an existing system. However, no matter how high-tech your system, even the best system is useless when you don't use it. Your security assessment should not only evaluate your alarm system, but also determine how often the system isn't armed when it should be. Alarm systems are great deterrents, but you still shouldn't rely entirely on one for your home's security. In reality, alarms notify the neighbors, alarm monitoring company and/or police after the burglar is already inside, and burglars know they typically have at least 10 minutes before law enforcement arrives. Remember, a good burglar can be in and out in 10 minutes or less. Be sure to analyze each layer of external security measures, as well as, you're your internal alert systems.

After you conduct a complete security audit of your home, share the results with your neighbors and encourage them to do the same with their homes. Explain any upgrades you made to your locks, doors, windows, lighting, etc. and the costs involved. Compare security systems with neighbors who already have one installed and encourage those who don't to get one. The more homes in the same neighborhood with an active security alarm with signs clearly displayed in the yards, the less likely burglars will target a house within that neighborhood. Another common avenue used to discourage criminals from targeting homes in a particular is starting a neighborhood watch program, such as those discussed in Chapter One. Read on for more detailed information about common security vulnerabilities you should evaluate for your home.

Keep Homes Under Lock and Key

As mentioned above, unlocked doors and windows are some of the most common ways burglars enter a home. They're also the quickest, quietest and easiest ways for burglars to get in and out undetected, and without expending any effort forcing their way inside. In short, your home will be an intruder's idea of child's play and hitting the jackpot rolled into one. Locking up is the most basic safety precaution you can take. Even when your leaving for "just a minute," lock your doors and windows anyway. This includes the car doors of any vehicles, even when they're left inside a locked garage. When you go to bed at night, engage every lock and set the alarm to protect you, your home and your family while everyone sleeps.

While there was a time when people didn't feel they needed to lock their homes, times have changed, and so have locks. The various mechanisms for securing doors and windows are a significant part of your overall home security strategy, but not all locks are created equal. Shopping for locks may quickly become overwhelming when you discover the many options available. While deadbolts emerged in the 1960s to provide additional security to a door, technological advances, such as electronic keyless locks, provide even more security enhancement to modern locking mechanisms. Reliable deadlocks and modern locks both have their place in securing your home.

When purchasing locks, there are three basic things to keep in mind: durability, key control and physical strength. Durability simply means you should only purchase high-quality locks guaranteed to survive years of use without becoming hard to operate or failing altogether. Key control can be a common oversight when you loan out your keys and someone makes a copy without your knowledge. It's fast, easy and typically inexpensive to get duplicate keys made at a number of locksmith shops and mass merchant stores. Consider having physical keys marked with "Do Not Duplicate" engravings; choose keyless locks and take precautions giving out the codes and change the codes often; or choose smart locks that allow you to remotely unlock doors from a smartphone application.

Finally, when considering physical strength, install high-quality, Grade 1 or 2 locks on every exterior door, including the door between the inside of an attached garage and interior of your home. These locks should resist prying and lock-picking attempts and could include deadbolts and/or keyed door knobs. Deadbolt locks should have beveled casings to inhibit intruders from shearing off lock cylinder pins and keyed knobs should contain mechanisms that prevent picking locks with credit cards, shims or similar items. Any lock should have bolts long enough to prevent doors from being pried open. Extra safety features of some locks also provide protection against sawing and drilling. This may include hardened outer material and/or inserts or anti-saw pins that make it more difficult to saw through bolts. Anti-drill protection uses internal, hardened steel chips that destroy drill bits when attempting to drill through the lock. Besides your front, back and garage doors, don't forget to secure exterior basement or cellar doors and all outbuildings with quality deadbolts.

Securing patio or sliding glass doors can be a bit trickier. These are often ideal points of entry, because these types of doors are inherently weak with latches instead of actual locks.

Defective latch mechanisms make them more vulnerable from being forced open. While you can limit movement by inserting a wooden dowel inside the door's track or installing track-blockers you can screw down, older sliding doors can simply be lifted and taken off the tracks. You can protect against this by installing a locking pin that extends through both the sliding and fixed portions of the sliding door or other types of auxiliary devices. However, even a thoroughly secured patio door can still be breached by simply breaking the glass for a quick "smash and grab" or when an intruder doesn't mind making a noisy entrance. Consider an impact-resistant sliding door replacement or install clear security window film. This film is a thin, protective sheet that isn't impenetrable, but does make glass harder to break through. Impact resistant glass and security film are also good options for windows in or near a door that could be broken and used to access the lock. Double cylinder deadbolts, which require a key to unlock them from either side, are another option, but can impede an emergency exit when keys aren't readily available and aren't permitted in some areas.

Safer Doors

Strong locks, however, are worthless when installed in poor quality doors or door frames. One of the most common ways to force entry into a home is by kicking open a door attached to a wooden jamb or frame. The weakest point of a door is most often where the strike plate holds the lock bolt in place at the jamb. Many plates are secured to the lightweight molding of the door frame, which are easily busted with a solid kick to the door near this plate. Upgrade to four-screw, reinforced strike plates installed with 3-4" screws that go deeper than the molding to the door frame stud beneath. These longer screws should also be used in a knob lock strike plate and at least one of the holes in each of the door's hinges.

Once you improve doorjamb security, evaluate the door itself. Replace weak, worn out or hollow core doors with solid wood, steel-wrapped wood-core or metal doors, which are much harder to break down. These doors should be at least 1 3/4" thick and fit the door frame securely. If you have exterior doors that swing out, be sure the hinge pins can't be easily removed and the door lifted off. While older doors might present a security risk, newer outswing doors commonly come with security style hinges that prevent removal of the door, even when the pins are removed or have distinct threaded pins that require a special tool for extraction. Finish off your safer exterior doors by mounting wide-angle, 160-degree peepholes or viewers no higher than 58 inches to identify visitors. You can also consider security cameras and/or motion sensor lights mounted above the doors and even a smart doorbell. You should never open a door without first checking to see who's on the other side, even when you're certain you know who it is. A bold robber (person who steals by gunpoint or another weapon while people are present) or home invader may walk right up and ring the doorbell for entry.

Safer Windows

While stronger doors increase the security of your home, windows often pose an even more enticing point of entry to intruders. First, windows are often overlooked and left unlocked more frequently than doors. Plus, windows typically have latches not locks, which can make them weak. Install secondary locking devices or replace latches with keyed locks, which are available for all types of windows. You can also install stops or through-the-frame lock pins that prevent a window from being raised no more than six inches. Locking pins lets you open a window for ventilation during warmer months while inhibiting intruders from slipping inside. Be sure this opening doesn't allow enough room to reach the pins and remove them.

While ground floor windows are obviously more susceptible to break-ins, upper floor windows can still be accessed by climbing nearby trees or trellising or utilizing a ladder that's been left out. You may be more inclined to leave an upper window wide open, thinking it's unreachable. All windows, both upper or lower, should be included in your home security alarm system and reinforced in some manner. You can make windows harder to break by installing security film similar to a sliding glass door. Also, consider replacing single pane windows with double-paned versions, which are harder to break and make your home more energy efficient. Grates, grills or bars over window offer added protection, but may not be quite the look you desire.

Besides safer windows, coverings for these windows not only add to your privacy, but can also be a deterrent to intruders. Similar to the window shopping you'd do at the mall, burglars do at your home. Install drapes, shades or other window treatments to keep tempting items out of a potential burglar's view. This is especially important at night when it's easier for burglars to scope out your home for potential items to steal. When you leave lights on inside your home at night with the blinds open, prowlers get a bird's eye view of all your treasures, your home's layout and its occupants. Discovering your home's layout and watching occupants also appeal to stalkers, rapists and peeping toms.

As a final added deterrent, each ground floor window or glass door should include highly visible decals. These decals should be placed near lock or latch mechanisms and should indicate the home is equipped with an alarm system and/ or has a security dog. Some might even announce that the neighborhood has a watch program.

Fixing Blind Spots in Landscaping

An unsecured ground floor window becomes even more attractive to burglars when nearby, overgrown vegetation conceals his presence. While you may use fencing and landscaping to add to your privacy, you could also inadvertently provide plenty of hiding places for prowlers. Sure, that row of hedges looks charming lining the side or front of your home, but it also makes a perfect place for concealment. Since visibility means vulnerability to a burglar, it's vital your security plan includes trimming back trees, shrubs and any vegetation that presents a blind spot or offers a hiding space. Plus, you don't want overgrown flora blocking your view of what's happening outside your home or concealing a break-in when you arrive home.

Hedges or bushes shouldn't be allowed to grow above waist level. Cut tree limbs near enough to easily reach upper level balconies and/or windows and rooftops, and remove lower branches next to your home that provide cover similar to a bush. Be especially brutal with the shears and loppers around doors, windows and porches. Taking away a burglar's cover is your first line of home defense. You can take it a step farther by only planting thorny plants, such as rose bushes, bougainvillea vines, holly or hawthorn trees, cacti or any flora that would be uncomfortable to hide behind. As part of your landscaping, you might also include gravel pathways or a gravel driveway that makes it harder for prowlers to conceal their footsteps.

When dealing with blind spots caused by landscaping, don't forget to assess any lighting issues. Even with well-trimmed bushes and trees, you can still have shadowed areas due to poor lighting choices and areas in complete dark due to no lighting whatsoever. You need to eliminate these hiding places, as well.

Better, Safer Lighting

Streetlights aren't the only way to increase safety in your neighborhood. Outside lighting is considered one of the best deterrents for keeping burglars at bay. Your security plan should include walking your property at night to identify areas in your yard that need better illumination. Eliminate shadows and dark areas that provide hiding places and compromise your safety. Also, light up specific areas around the perimeter of your house, including all entryways, driveways and pathways, for safety and security.

Flood lights offer the maximum in security with light cast across a wide area that discourages intruders. Mounting flood lights about nine feet high makes them harder for prowlers to reach. Besides strategically-placed floods, avoid overly bright lights that can surprisingly cause a negative effect by creating undesirable patches of deep shadow. Instead, consider an outdoor lighting plan that provides soft, overall landscape lighting that eliminates dark areas and hiding places.

Add motion-detecting sensors to flood lights and other landscaping lights around your property. This helps when you don't want certain lights on all the time and also alerts you when someone is in your yard after dark. Plus, the sudden change from dark to light not only gives you a visual alert, it can also startle intruders and make them more likely to run away. Motion activated lights placed in various areas around your yard make it easier to notice and track someone moving about. You can also install more sophisticated motion sensors that detect body heat.

Moving indoors, interior lighting indicates signs of activity inside. This makes light timers ideal in making your home appear occupied while you're away at night. A darkened home, especially one that's dark for several nights in a row when you're on vacation or extended trip out of town, lets burglars know the house is empty. Use your timers every day, not just when you're out of town. This way, neighbors are used to the light show and will become suspicious, if your house is suddenly plunged into darkness. Install timers on lights near the front and rear windows of your house, but still keep your curtains closed. You can also use timers on televisions and radios to further promote your illusion of occupancy, but set the volume at a level it won't set off any audio sensors you might have on your alarm system.

Smart timers are also available that allow remote programming from your cellphone.

Other Security Enhancements

There are a multitude of other things you can do to improve the security of your home. This includes simple things like always changing the locks when you move to a new home or bigger endeavors like acquiring a trained security dog for added protection. There are also several other ways to prevent burglars from knowing your house is empty while you're away.

Turn down the volume of your landline phone's ringer, so it can't be heard from outside. Prowlers near your home hear the phone isn't being picked up and realize no one's home. If possible, have your calls forwarded, because some burglars might call to see whether you're at home, prior to breaking in. If this makes you wonder how burglars would get your phone number, it's quite simple. If your number is listed and your name is on your mailbox, then all they (and stalkers) have to do is look you up in the phonebook or online.

If you're going to be gone for an extended period of time, don't forget to arrange to have your lawn moved in the summer and snow removed from your walkways in the winter. Ask a neighbor to pick up your mail and newspapers, instead of having them stopped, so potential burglars see deliveries still being made. Anytime you're away from home, even for a short while, never leave notes on your door. You could also ask neighbors to park in your driveway to make it look like someone's home or to use your trash can occasionally and put it out on the curb on trash day.

Speaking of trash day, when you get a new, expensive toy, don't advertise it to the whole world by putting the box out by the curb before trash day. You'll most likely want to discard boxes from most valuable items, especially large electronics. However, by adding them to your curbside trash immediately, a potential burglar now knows exactly what new big-ticket items are available for the taking. Keep the great loot inside your house a secret by stashing boxes inside your garage or other indoor area until garbage day, then take it out as the garbage truck arrives. Better yet, break down the boxes and take them to a recycling center.

Always let your neighbors know when you'll be gone for a while. If you've done a good job of making friends with people in your neighborhood, then they shouldn't mind keeping an eye on things for you. Be sure to authorize them to report any suspicious activity they see to your neighborhood watch group and/or the local police department.

Be a Good Neighbor

Along with all the security measures you can take around your property, some of the best security comes simply from being a good neighbor. Neighbors who look out for one another is one of the best crime prevention tools you can utilize. This concept is simple, just get to know your neighbors, especially those closet to you. Once you establish a good relationship with nearby residents, they're often willing to watch out for your home and help with small tasks, as long as you return the favor. Tasks may include making your home look occupied while you're out of town or holding on to a spare set of keys.

When you find a neighbor you trust with your keys, it solves the dilemma of where to safely keep them that's still close enough for emergency lockouts or when service people need inside and you're not available.

It's unfortunate that police officers can't be everywhere at once, but you and your fellow residents usually know what's going on in your neighborhood. This helps you be the eyes and ears for law enforcement when they can't be there. To build the best network, get to know your neighborhood's beat officers as well as your adjacent neighbors, and establish relationships built on trust and a commitment to keep the neighborhood safe.

Even if your entire neighborhood participates in a crime watch program, develop your own mini-neighborhood crime watch with the residents closest to your house. Your close-knit group of watchers further sends a message to intruders that someone is on alert and it creates a stronger sense of responsibility for protecting everyone's property as if it were your own. If your neighborhood doesn't have a watch program established, consider starting one by contacting your local police department. They can help you plan and organize a watch program appropriate for your neighborhood, and even help recruit members in some cases.

Neighborhood safety is a team effort and communication is a key element, so talk often. Be sure your group knows when one of you will be gone for more than the day and whether there are any small tasks that need completed during this absence. However, don't just communicate when you're leaving town or need a favor. Learn important details, such as work and school schedules, whether there are small children or elderly occupants that might need looking after, descriptions of friends and family that visit frequently or aren't allowed to visit at all and other notable issues everyone in the group should know.

Develop a phone tree to alert others of potential problems or ask questions when you're not sure whether a car or person belongs in the neighborhood. Plus, make sure you have a way to reach any neighbors who're gone, so you can inform them of anything amiss they should know about right away. You might also contact them, if you see something out of the ordinary at their house you're unsure about. They may clear up confusion about who should be there while they're away before unnecessarily involving the police, or commission you to contact the authorities for them, if they're concerned about what you witnessed.

Whenever you see something or someone that's truly suspicious around you or your neighbor's home, call the police immediately. This includes when anyone's home is broken into. If you believe the intruder is still inside the house or another genuine emergency arises, don't hesitate to dial 9-1-1. Never go inside a house where an intruder might be lurking or confront a criminal who could react in a violent manner. Instead, wait outside until help arrives, even when you're worried about your possessions. Insurance should cover any items stolen, so it's not worth risking your life. Anytime you can do so without putting yourself in danger, make note of license plate numbers of suspicious vehicles, detailed descriptions of vehicles and suspects and route of escape to pass along to police officers.

Remember, if something looks wrong, never be afraid to say something.

"The one thing that I would like to say and I think unfortunately is not said enough or acted on enough is, 'we're all responsible for our own safety and security,'" said a VP of Guest Services. "People forget that they have power and their powers are their eyes, their ears and their mouth, and they get to say things and they get to observe things. It is so important that we all take an active role in making our home safe, our community safe and not just pass the buck to somebody else to do. If you see something isn't right, you need to say something."

You know your neighborhood, put that knowledge to work by using your eyes and ears to spot trouble and then call your local police. Law enforcement officers are trained and dedicated to protecting their community and its citizens. Residents working in cooperation with local police make one of the best crime-fighting teams, so take an active role in protecting your neighborhood, which in turn provides greater security for your home.

Install a Security System

According to a 2013 study by North Carolina at Charlotte's Department of Criminal Justice and Criminology, approximately 83 percent of the professional burglars they surveyed said they try to determine whether an alarm existed before they attempted a burglary. If there was an alarm at their intended target, 60 percent said they would seek an alternative target. Burglars who spend time carefully planning a burglary made up a large part of this group and were most likely to skip homes with complex security systems.

However, like any other security precaution, an alarm system only works when it's properly installed and armed. While a burglar might bypass your home due to a sophisticated security system, you must also learn how to use your advanced system. You'll need adequate training to understand complex operating instructions, use your system to its fullest potential and perform or schedule routine maintenance to ensure it continues working accurately.

Alarm systems increase the potential of a burglar being caught, especially when the system includes surveillance camera components. At the very least, alarm systems with audible sirens will often scare intruders away before they complete their criminal tasks. Plus, home alarm systems can also monitor other sensors, such as fire and carbon monoxide, and panic buttons.

Speaking of sensors, consider the various sensors and other equipment available for whole house protection that add extra layers of protection indoors when your outer layers have been breached. While standard systems include door and window sensors to trip the alarm when one is opened, motion and/or noise detectors and glass-break sensors are nice augmentations to your alarm system. Some sensors sound the alarm when burglars attempt to bypass window sensors by breaking a window instead of opening it to gain access. Others can detect motion when an intruder gains access from an open window, which doesn't require forced entry that would normally set off the alarm.

It's beneficial to install motion detection sensors outdoors, as well. These sensors alert you when someone is moving around your yard at times when no one is home, so you can check on your home and evaluate the situation immediately using a smartphone app or similar device. Since many burglaries take place during the daytime while most people are away at work or school, these alerts help you keep an eye on your property throughout the day when neighbors who normally watch your property might also be away. Outdoor motion sensors should be lighted, so they not only detect movement, but also turn on flood lighting to more easily see someone approaching your home after dark.

Due to advances in home security solutions, criminals can also be caught on camera. Security cameras with live video feeds provide visual verification there's an intruder in your home, so police respond quickly and may catch the criminal at the scene. These cameras can also catch the crime on recorded video. Live and recorded images assist in catching and potentially prosecuting perpetrators, which make burglars think twice about hitting your home. Invest in high definition cameras, so captured photo or video images are clear enough to provide a better quality picture of the perpetrator and aid in easier identification.

To get the most out of a security system, install one that not only rings on site, but also to a remote location that's monitored round-the-clock by a security company with a UL Listed Central Station or preferably a UL Listed CSAA 5 Diamond Certified Central Station. Always make sure your response call list is up to date, so monitoring companies and/or emergency responders can quickly reach you. Also, be sure your audible alarm automatically resets after a couple of minutes, so neighbors won't have to listen to the bell until it's shut off. Once the audible alarm sounds, burglars know they've tripped it and will hopefully flee. It also alerts your neighborhood watch group to be alert for potential suspects or vehicles that leave the area quickly.

When choosing a securing system be sure to choose a system that has a backup battery and using GSM (Global System for Mobile) radio. This will protect your home during power loss and GSM communication eliminates the need for a costly land line from your phone company. Then, display yard signs and stickers alerting potential intruders there's a system installed, which could dissuade them from targeting your home from the outset. These notices should be visible from every entry point of your home and not just the front entrance. While you may feel these signs are unsightly, having them on display is a vital burglary deterrent.

Although a home security system doesn't guarantee your home won't be burglarized, displayed signs that indicate it'll be difficult to enter your home unnoticed can lower the threat of crime. Plus, many insurance providers offer discounts when you install security upgrades, especially an alarm system. To keep your security pass code safe, never post it near the alarm key pad and only share it with those you trust. If your security code has fallen into the hands of an untrustworthy person, change it immediately.

Since criminals are getting more professional and sophisticated, to help guarantee your home's safety, you must do the same. An alarm system is one of the biggest ways to discourage burglars from targeting your home. There are a variety of alarm options to meet various budgets and security needs. While it's advisable to have your system professionally installed, it's possible to set up a do-it-yourself system. However, these systems do have a much higher risk of operating errors and system failure from improper installation, which may not provide the protection you expect when you need it most.

DIY vs Pro Install

Whatever security system you choose, proper installation is vital to ensure it functions satisfactorily and provides the safety features you need every time you need them. While DIY installations are cheaper, professional installations are not only easier, but also more reliable. Plus, professional installers can often provide additional safety tips for your home and detailed information on how to properly use and maintain your system. When you DIY your security system, you may worry that everything might not work correctly, but professional installers make sure each component is working as it should. Let's rundown some of the pros and cons of DIY versus professional installation.

Although there are some benefits to DIY installation, there are a number of major drawbacks. The biggest benefit when you install your security system yourself is obviously the money you'll save on installation fees. Besides this money savings, when you choose a company that offers DIY systems, you typically own the equipment, so if you move, your equipment goes with you, without an equipment relocation fee. This often appeals to renters or people whose jobs require them to move around frequently. You also have the luxury of installing the system on your own schedule, instead of waiting for an appointment with an installer.

During the actual installation, many homeowners find wireless DIY systems fairly easy to install with either electronic prompts or verbal walkthroughs during installation. However, the professional you talk with over the phone during setup can't see the inside of your home and won't be able to make certain recommendations that an on-site installer could. Plus, if you prefer a hard-wired system, you could find these much trickier to install, especially if you're not a handy person. The need for an easy to install system can severely limit your options.

If you're not a security expert, one major drawback of a DIY installation is the lingering doubts you might have over whether your equipment and system are set up correctly. Plus, if you successfully get your system installed, you'll now have to teach yourself how to use it. If you're technology savvy, this might not be too disconcerting, but otherwise, the lack of technical guidance might be rather daunting. With a professional installation, company representatives walk through the entire system with you and explain in detail how to use each feature.

Going back to the money you saved with a DIY install, you may end up paying more for your equipment, because you miss out on discounts for package deals. Worse, you might not qualify for certain warranties, because there's no guarantee you installed the system correctly. This could cost you big time! If your home is burglarized or damaged by fire, your insurance company may refuse your claim when there's doubt about whether the system was installed right. When your system is professionally installed, the security company takes on this liability.

While a professional install requires an installation fee, your biggest benefit is not having to worry about making a mistake during the installation process. Professionals ensure your system is set up properly and can answer all your technical questions. You benefit from and should take advantage of, their vast knowledge and experience. While this service does come with a price tag, companies often include cost-saving incentives when you pay for professional installations, such as discounted equipment or package upgrades.

One drawback is any potential stipulations should you decide to move to a new home. This could require a second installation fee to move your equipment or leaving some of your equipment behind and/or having to purchase new equipment. Other drawbacks do include rearranging your schedule to have your equipment installed during a set appointment time and potentially having less control over your system setup. However, the peace of mind you receive from knowing your security system was set up for peak performance often outweighs these inconveniences.

In the end, installing your own security system can potentially save you money and help avoid scheduling conflicts. However, when you forego professional installation, you run a big risk of making a mistake that causes you to experience an undetected break-in or fire. Faulty installations put both your home and your family at risk. Furthermore, a DIY system may be much more prone to false alarms. This could cost you much more than you saved on the installation fee when you receive a stiff fine from the police department.

The Rising Concern Over False Alarms

Poorly installed or maintained security systems and insufficient knowledge of how an alarm system works can cause significant problems, not only for home or business owners, but also local police. Over the years, the use of security alarms has increased, but at the same time, legitimate calls have become less frequent and false alarms are the norm. The growing number of false alarms forced many police departments to handle burglar alarms differently, including severe ramifications to both business and residential security alarm users.

One direct result of the high rate of false alarms was the passing of ordinances by local governments that penalized repeat false alarm offenders. In some cases, even first-time offenders can receive large fines in an attempt to combat wasted resources. While these fines are one way to recoup expenses, the charges typically only cover a small fraction of the costs associated with responding to an alarm. Around the country, law enforcement agencies spend millions of dollars and thousands of labor hours every year responding to alarms mistakenly triggered in homes and businesses. Plus, responding to these false alarms take police away from real emergencies.

Many security alarm companies report that 70% of the alarms they receive are false and large city police departments report that between 95-98% of the alarms they respond to are false. These numbers make security systems appear unreliable and less credible. However, a large chunk of these false alarms are simply due to operator error. Another significant portion is caused by improper installation and/or maintenance of the system. The fear of false alarms makes some residents reluctant to even arm their system, which then exposes their property to undetected theft and fire. Instead of putting your home and family at risk, realize the most common causes of residential false alarms and takes the appropriate steps to eliminate them.

Again, one of the biggest culprits of false alarms is operator error. This may not mean you specifically, but could include others who have access to your alarm. This may be immediate and extended family members, domestic help, child/pet/house sitters, lawn care professionals or anyone allowed access to your alarm. Be sure each person is adequately trained on how to use the system, especially how to cancel the alarm should it activate falsely. If you used a professional installer, you should have received thorough training on the proper use of your system and you should use this knowledge to mitigate operator errors.

Professional installers also ensure your system is installed correctly, which can help eliminate equipment malfunctions. They also provide you with general maintenance tasks, such as checking for weak or depleted batteries, which can also cause your system to misfire.

If your system includes motion sensors, be sure they're set at the appropriate level, so wandering pets don't activate the alarm. You'll also want to test the sensitivity level of motion detectors to ensure it doesn't respond to the slightest stimuli, such as drafts from heating/air conditioning systems that cause a plant or curtain to sway.

Loose-fitting or defective doors and windows can also cause drafts that could trigger an alarm. However, they might also set off alarms when they rattle in their casement and make the system think someone is trying to break in. Inspect and repair faulty windows and doors during your vulnerability assessment. This potentially helps prevent false alarms, while it also removes weak areas that could attract intruders and increases your home's energy efficiency.

These are a few steps you can take to lower your risk of being guilty of a false alarm. Before activating your system, however, find out if your city requires a home alarm system permit. While police officers typically still respond in the usual manner to burglar alarms without a required permit on file, you'll likely not only face a false alarm fine, but also a severe penalty for operating an alarm without the proper permit.

While officers feel duty-bound to investigate all calls, many law enforcement agencies rank burglar alarms as a low priority. This means it could be quite some time before an officer arrives to investigate your alarm. Your city may have also adopted Verified Response Protocols. This means police officers won't respond to an alarm, unless it's been verified through activated audio and/or video surveillance or eyewitness accounts that confirm a crime is either occurring or has occurred. Some cities also utilize mandatory alarm training school for repeat offenders.

"Each municipality or department is a little different," commented one police commander, "but I must say, our department as a larger department has ordinances. If you get so many false alarms, you'll get charged for them. People tend to get the sensitivity adjusted on their alarms."

"When we {receive an} alarm," he continued, "we respond like it's real, unless we have reason to believe otherwise. However, if you have video verification that someone is in the house, you're not just getting two officers coming. Everyone's coming. We need to get this bad guy, because you don't break into just one house a month or year, you break into ten or twelve a week minimum. We have everyone come, set up a perimeter, see the vehicles in the driveway and who is involved. We treat each false alarm like it's real, but with video verification that's another layer of confirmation and validation. It's not just two officers, it might be ten officers coming."

Don't be guilty of wasting valuable police resources. Ensure your alarm is properly installed and maintained. Then, make sure you and everyone else who touches it knows how to use it. If you've outgrown a standard security system, you might be interested in how technology has further changed home security.

Advanced Home Security Options

Advances in technology change everything, including how you protect your home. The digital revolution has made what you previously thought was only possible in science fiction movies, a reality in your own house. Security options have gotten smarter and more streamlined to fit a variety of needs and technological levels.

While it may seem new to you, remote monitoring has become a common item included in a home security system. This allows you to keep an eye on your home from anywhere with real-time videos and/or photos. These monitoring systems also often give you the ability to arm and disarm your security system, stream your security camera feeds and send intruder or fire alerts remotely from your current location. They're also handy if your police department requires verification of a crime prior to sending units to investigate.

"Smart" technology offers a lot of options for your home, as well. This includes smart door locks, which can detect your presence using your smartphone's Bluetooth to unlock doors for you automatically. Advanced smart locks can also "talk" to other connected devices in a home automation system, and may be a safer option for physical keys that could get lost or fall into the wrong hands. While Bluetooth locks have fewer features than Wi-Fi locks, they're a more secure option, due to Wi-Fi locks' increased vulnerability to online security breaches. An even more secure door locking system, however, comes in the form of fingerprint door locks. While these are still in the infant stage, they are becoming more widely used and are quickly gaining momentum.

You can also go utterly high-tech with a complete home automation system. These systems allow you to control almost anything in your home from any location. This allows you to turn your smartphone or tablet into a long distance remote control for locks, lights, garage doors, appliances, thermostats, security cameras or any smart home device you have connected to your system. Smart home automation systems conveniently control various aspects of your home, including better control of your security system.

The Bottom Line

Once you've done everything inside and out to make your home a safer, more secure environment for you and your family, remember to stay alert to threats and be smart. Whether you have an alarm system or not, never enter your home when you notice your door has been jimmied or a window broken. The intruder could still be inside and it can be dangerous to confront a criminal. Call the police immediately for assistance, then stay outside or go to a nearby neighbor's house to wait.

While it's important to improve your home's security, don't exchange security for you and your family's personal safety. If you make you fortify home too much, you might inadvertently also make it difficult to get out, which could hamper your escape should there be a fire or another emergency. Although the overall point of your vulnerability assessment is to make your home more burglar-resistant, a good assessment shouldn't solely focus on crime. It should also include threats posed by fires and natural and man-made disasters. Your overall security strategy should include appropriate evacuation procedures to help your family quickly get out, while preventing intruders from easily getting in.

Boosting residential security doesn't have to be a big-budget project, there are many things you can do yourself, but others that are best left to professionals. No matter the expense, however, the safety of your home and your family should be worth any price.

Crime costs businesses billions of dollars each year and can be a big factor in business' failure. During tough economic times, it's common for criminal activity to increase and your business must be safeguarded accordingly. Your business may already be susceptible to a variety of crimes, so increasing security helps guard against the impact this criminal activity has on your profitability. Small businesses are particularly vulnerable to crime, largely due to limited security budgets. These limitations make it difficult to have the proper components in place to detect and prevent crime.

While some crimes against businesses are actually committed by its employees, I'll be addressing crimes committed outside the company. These crimes include property crimes, such as burglary, robbery, shoplifting, arson and vandalism, and computer hacking or cybercrime.

Despite their smaller revenues, small businesses are often actually bigger targets for property crimes, which is largely due to a lack of proper security measures. While a deficiency in funds to invest in security equipment plays a large role, small business owners might also falsely believe their business doesn't bring in enough money to catch the eye of a thief. When in fact, criminals seek easy targets, even if the payoff is smaller, because their chances of getting away with the crime are greatly increased.

The security and safety of your business begins with a hard look at your security strategies. You not only need to evaluate the physical layout but also your current security equipment and methods, to discover and correct inadequacies. You'll need to provide training for your entire staff on how to protect the business and themselves from crime, and cover all the security procedures you want them to follow. While some criminals will "case" a business and decide when, how or whether to strike, most crimes are crimes of opportunity. If you fail to take appropriate security precautions, you invite crime into your business.

CHAPTER 4

||||||||||||||||||||||||||||||||||||||||||||||

Business and Crime Prevention

There are four main prevention strategies you can use -- developmental, community, criminal justice and situational prevention. Developmental involves examining the root causes of crimes against businesses and will require some research on your part. Community strategies can utilize a variety of neighborhood and/or business watch programs and also demands you get more involved with your community. Criminal justice includes reaching out to local law enforcement for guidance on ways to keep your business safe and to establish a good relationship with the beat officers that patrol your neighborhood. Finally, situational prevention is critical and includes surveillance techniques through security alarm systems, video monitoring, environmental design and properly trained employees.

Police and Community Outreach

You don't want fear of crime to isolate your business, because this can further increase your vulnerability to crime. It takes a community effort to help reduce and prevent crime, which helps protect small businesses. This requires you to reach out to the community as a whole, and local law enforcement. Police personnel can work with you to improve security and change the design of your space to reduce the risk of crime. Similar to a Neighborhood Watch, you can also join with other small business owners to form a Business Watch. This prompts members to watch over every business as if it were their own and alert each other and the proper authorities about any suspicious activity and/or patterns of crime witnessed. As a business owner you should also become more involved with local schools, youth groups, churches and civic organizations to help combat drug-related activity, violence and other crimes to create a safer community for everybody.

To start, contact your local police and/or sheriff's department to conduct a security survey of your business. They can point out weak spots and offer advice on locks, alarms and every potential vulnerability. Once they help you appropriately secure your property, ask about starting a Business Watch. Modeled after the Neighborhood Watch program, these programs train business owners and their staff to be the eyes and ears for police when they'd can't physically be there. These groups also establish a link between various small businesses and law enforcement. Your watch group might partner with community groups, as well, for added assistance in reducing commercial crime within the neighborhood.

A Business Watch requires you to get to know other business owners in your area. One, or sometimes several, police officer(s) may be assigned as a liaison to your group and the group may elect a business leader to act as the block's security administrator to represent all the participating businesses. A phone tree and/or radios are useful for businesses to stay linked to each other and law enforcement partners. Crime prevention officers will help train business owners/operators and their employees in how to effectively observe and report crimes and suspicious activities. They also teach you to remove easy crime opportunities to prevent robberies and burglaries and which security measures work best to detect, impede and potentially catch criminals. You'll learn valuable self-protection methods, so you recognize dangerous situations and understand how to avoid, prevent or flee from these situations.

Your group should also take part in the Operation Identification (ID) program. This involves marking or engraving all your equipment, machines, tools and other valuable property with a traceable, identifying number. This number could be any unique number, such as your license or tax identification number. Don't forget to keep an up-to-date inventory sheet of these items locked up somewhere safe off the premises. This program helps deter crime and lets law enforcement identify lost or stolen property and return it to its rightful owner. Each participating business displays Operation ID and Business Watch decals on doors and windows to discourage burglary or other theft.

Getting civic organizations and other community groups involved can also help continue the watch once businesses are closed. Looking for community partners should start with your Chamber of Commerce, who often help implement a Business Watch and provides crime prevention information to all area businesses. Many communities also have local chapters of service clubs, such as Lions, Kiwanis, Junior Service League, Jaycees, Rotary and etc., who often have members from local businesses, willing to partner in a Business Watch program. You might also find effective partnerships with community and neighborhood associations, including Neighborhood Watch and Park Watch groups. One last line of defense is utilizing private security to enhance efforts to protect commercial zones. Even with an aggressive Business Watch group, small business security technology is critical in the fight against crime.

Surveillance and Camera Security

Environmental design programs as part of your situational prevention can be an easy way to improve the security of your business. These programs utilize structural design methods for the exterior of your building and appropriate interior layouts. Besides lack of a security system, adequate hiding places are one of the biggest advantages for criminals seeking easy targets. If you remove hiding places from your business design, it's harder for criminals to surprise on-duty employees or sneak up on security guards you employ either during or after business hours. They're also more visible to surveillance cameras. Your best strategy to defend against crime should always have a strong focus on surveillance and camera security, including remote viewing capabilities. Simple actions like improving security lighting, installing new locks or updating an alarm system frequently reduces crime.

Camera security systems aren't usually anything like what you expect. Security camera footage on television shows and in movies is often depicted as high quality, high resolution video and audio. The investigators can blow it up, freeze it frame-by-frame and extract the tiniest detail about a crime. This is rarely true in real life. Small Mom and Pop stores tend to have very little money left over to invest in expensive monitoring devices or state of the art security and camera systems. Instead, they tend to make do with the cheapest cameras available, or purchase used, outdated technology that still utilize recording discs that they reuse over and over until the results are filled with ghostly images of previous recordings. The reality of most small business' security footage is images that are dark and/or blurry at best, and the quality never decent enough to identify a criminal. The inability to properly monitor and record criminal activity puts these businesses at higher risk of various property crimes and reinforces the need for updated technology.

"I can't stress enough what video surveillance does," said one Police Department Commander. "A silent alarm with a video where the guy has his picture taken and he's being videoed before he realizes it . . . I can't stress enough how many crimes are solved that way. If a police officer hasn't come in contact with him and doesn't recognized him, the public usually does. Especially the neighborhood. Someone recognizes this knuckle head. Even with the way they walk or the way thy carry themselves or what they say, if you also have audio on the camera."

"We have had homicide scenes where the cameras are perfectly positioned," he continued, "but they're old cameras or the tape has literally been in there for a year . . . the whole thing has been videoed, but it's all snow. You send it away and now it's half snow, but it's snow nonetheless. That doesn't help us. But these new digital cameras are relatively cheap and have storage on the cloud . . . it really is a godsend. It's like DNA. It's the new DNA. We encourage everyone to update and upgrade. If they don't have one, get one."

So, how often do private video surveillance systems either in businesses or even someone's home help law enforcement solve a case?

"Put it this way," explained the commander, "If you don't have video, we go to the neighbors that do. We might not catch the crime, but we'll catch the person coming up and leaving, and we'll have to use inductive reasoning and realize this has to be the guy or gal that did such and such. In this day and age, you can click on YouTube and watch the video or click your smartphone and see who is in your house {or business}. It'll give you an alert, you can see who is in {there} . . . and why are they there. Literally, if you have the right technology, it'll help 95 percent of the time. It's rare that you have someone who's a professional burglar from out of state. It's just not the case."

There are many types of business security systems available and you may choose to utilize more than one to fully protect your property. These could include video surveillance, intrusion detection alarm, and electronic access control systems. With increased cases of cybercrime, you should also invest in computer security systems.

Your video surveillance system should include live video and in some instances perhaps audio feeds. These systems help protect both the interior and exterior of your business, including the surrounding area outside. Video surveillance utilizes cameras mounted in and around your business and are often integrated with web or mobile devices, so you can see what's happening 24/7. This allows you to not only monitor for break-ins after closing, but also watch customers and employees during business hours to detect shoplifting or employee theft. Since these systems also record live feeds, you'll have video proof of any illegal activity should you need to file a police report or insurance claim. There are many vendors who install the necessary cameras and set up the software needed to record data feeds. These companies usually charge initial installation and/or equipment fees and a monthly fee for service and/or monitoring of the system. While this costs more than installing a system yourself, professional installation helps guarantee it's done correctly and lowers the chance of system failures and false alarms.

Many business owners add intrusion detection alarms to their surveillance system. These alarms typically include several different devices and sensors to detect entry from doors and/or windows. This could include motion detectors and glass breaking sensors that are typically monitored by a professional, third-party vendor who receives an alert for any unauthorized access and immediately calls the business to determine whether police dispatch is required. These systems come with a keypad for arming/disarming, so you must thoroughly train employees responsible for opening and/or closing on how to use it.

Like residential burglar alarm systems, the growing cost and concern over false alarms, caused some cities to adopt policies against dispatching officers to unconfirmed commercial burglar alarms or placing these calls on a lower priority. This is where video surveillance further comes into play when you can confirm an intruder from live video and/or audio feeds. Remember, professionally installed systems help guarantee they're installed correctly and maintained properly.

Electronic access control systems can also be utilized to protect certain rooms that should only be accessed by authorized personnel. This system is helpful for cash offices or any room where there is sensitive or proprietary information you want to keep out of the wrong hands. These systems are typically simple, but can include uncomplicated keypad entry mechanisms tied to individual doors or large, networked systems with access cards you swipe to enter various areas throughout the building. Although many small businesses wouldn't necessarily need this type of system, electronic key code systems do safeguard against terminated employees and take away the worry over lost keys, since a new code could be re-programmed at any time.

Lastly, if you have important business files or documents that contain sensitive company and customer information or other critical information saved on your computer system, it's critical to protect it from cybercrime. Security breaches caused by computer hacking has run rampant in recent years and hackers are surprisingly starting to target smaller companies the same as large corporations. A good computer security program, however, doesn't just protect your company from hackers, it also protects you from spyware, viruses and other cyber threats.

Damage to your computer system could not only cost you hours of lost productivity, it could have a significant effect on your customer base should they fear their information may be compromised while in your hands. It is incredibly important to invest in a firewall and have it set up by a certified network engineer. It will be a small investment when measured against the time and cost associated from cleaning up the damage caused by a hacker. At the very least, invest in a reliable, and up-to-date antivirus software to prevent viruses from entering your network. Antivirus security is often a low cost safety measure that only requires a nominal yearly subscription fee.

Remember any alarm system you install should be maintained properly and regularly. Each system should have a fail-safe battery backup in case your business loses power or power is cut by intruders. Your alarm system should also have fire-sensing capabilities to alert the proper authorities should there be a fire, including arson attempts, on the premises either during or after hours. If you're unsure what type(s) of security system is right for your business, discuss it with a reputable security consultant or ask your local law enforcement agency to perform a security survey for you.

Overnight Security

If you have continual problems with crime in your neighborhood, besides a state of the art security system, you might also decide to step up overnight security procedures. Overnight security doesn't just entail hiring security personnel to patrol your property. It should also include physical techniques to aid in thwarting burglars and other intruders.

The more difficult and risky you make their criminal activity, the less likely they will target and/or penetrate your business.

Like residential security, a business owner's first line of defense is to take away hiding places and keep all windows and doors locked up tight with the alarm system armed after the business closes. Similar to home security, protect windows with clear security film or clear polycarbonate sheets. You can also opt for grill work, grates or bars over windows, but these can be disconcerting to customers. While it's more expensive, unbreakable safety glass can be a more attractive, less off-putting option. Glass doors should be treated similarly and security doors should be metal-lined with metal security crossbars securing them. These doors should also be under the eye of a surveillance camera to allow staff inside to see who's outside the door prior to opening it.

All external locks should be of the highest quality, including padlocks on overhead and receiving doors. Be sure the hasps holding the padlocks are securely bolted to a metal plate and bolts are concealed when the hasp is shut and padlocked in place. As an added precaution, remove serial numbers from locks to prevent intruders from matching them with a key or having a key made that fits that particular lock. Potential entrance points often overlooked include ventilation ducts, skylights and fire escapes. You can protect ducts and skylights with metal grates or bars and the first stair on a fire escape should not be reachable from the ground.

Businesses also have to practice good key control. This means keeping a log for keys checked out to employees and restrict access to keys to only your most trusted employees.

Always engrave "Do Not Duplicate" on keys and re-key every door when an employee quits or is terminated from their position. If you have a high turnover rate, it could be more cost effective to install an electronic key code access system.

Burglary is one of the biggest overnight threats to a business and even with all these precautions in place, a burglar may still target your business. If you've had a good alarm system properly installed and it was armed after the business closed, then it should go off. Either way, there are other steps you can take to further deter crime, potentially catch the intruder and safeguard money left overnight.

Appropriate security lighting is one of the best crime deterrents. Externally, light up any dark areas, especially around windows and doors. After hours, leave some lights on up front, so you can clearly see indoors. Keep front, display windows uncluttered and use low counters and open spaces, so burglars can't easily hide once inside. Expensive merchandise should be completely removed from display windows at night. Place your cash register(s) and safe up front, so the thief's activities is visible from outside. Keep cash register drawers open, so it's obvious they're empty and burglars won't be tempted to bust them open. Although it's best to not leave money overnight, if you keep cash on the premises after closing, always lock it in your safe, which should be anchored in concrete with a combination lock. If your safe is empty, leave it open, as well.

Anyone who opens the store should never enter the building if it looks like there's been a breach. Not only could the intruder still be inside, they can unwittingly tamper with evidence. Call the police immediately and wait outside for their arrival.

While robberies don't frequently occur, they can be much more dangerous, because they could involve physical violence to those present during the event. This could be employees and customers. Eliminate blind spots where robbers can hide before springing on unwitting employees or during the commission of their crime. Just like burglary prevention, you want your business well-lit and the front windows clear of displays or signage, so passersby can witness what's going on inside and hopefully call the police. Consider installing a panic button near cash registers when contemplating your security system. These buttons should ring directly to your local police station. To reduce monetary loss, only keep small amounts of cash in registers and utilize a drop safe for large bills and excess money. Clearly post that money is dropped regularly and cashiers don't have access to these safes. Make daily deposits to keep on-hand cash as low as possible, but never take the same route to the bank and take an escort when possible. In the event of a robbery, always cooperate, because merchandise and cash can be replaced, but people cannot. Ask your police liaison to schedule a training session to brief employees on what to do in case there's a robbery.

While shoplifting doesn't typically affect a business' safety, businesses do lose billions of dollars every year to this crime. To help deter this activity, keep expensive items locked in display cases. Merchandise should never be kept near exits to prevent snatch and run situations. Train employees how to reduce shoplifting opportunities and what to do when they suspect it's taking place, including rules on apprehension. Strategically-placed mirrors can eliminate blind spots and help spot criminal activity. You may want to install an electronic inventory control system that activates when merchandise not properly deactivated nears an exit.

Likewise, vandalism isn't necessarily a security threat to a business, but again it's a costly crime nonetheless. Many vandals are younger persons, but any act of vandalism should still be reported. Damage from vandalism should be cleaned/covered up right away. Discourage vandals with hard-to-mark surfaces, fences, lighting and landscape designs utilizing prickly hedges and shrubs. Hold community meetings, including police liaisons, to discuss ongoing vandalism and find solutions and prevention efforts that benefit everyone.

A final option to enhanced security and safety of your small business is hiring professional security personnel. The mere presence of a uniformed guard is often a large deterrent to crime, both from outside and internal sources. The investment in this service is often recouped through crime, shoplifting and employee theft deterrence. While your business is closed, knowing someone is actively guarding your establishment also gives you added peace of mind. If your company can't afford the upfront cost of hiring a security company, join with neighboring businesses to share the expense and have rotating patrols between participating businesses. You can opt to contract with a reputable security company or employ your own private security staff.

Employee Training and Protocol

Many of your business' safety and security measures won't be as effective, if you don't provide adequate training to your employees. This includes proper safety procedures to not only keep the business safe, but also themselves, fellow employees and customers. Protocol for employee safety is even more important than the safety of business assets. Again, people can't be replaced, but monetary and physical goods are frequently covered by insurance policies. Call on your police liaison(s) to offer educational presentations to your employees, so they're better equipped with appropriate crime prevention techniques and tactics.

"As far as the training people," explained a police department commander, "you can contact your local law enforcement and they usually have a training staff, who will come out and talk to you. They can do a PowerPoint demonstration . . . They will show you what's bad, what's good, what to look out for, what you can and can't do, what you should and should not confront. Even with employees, you have an employee who is all of the sudden radicalized or all of the sudden upset about something, disgruntled, you want to deescalate that before it gets to the point of no return. You don't have to be a radical terrorist or anything, it could just be someone at the edge going through a divorce, losing his kids, got in a traffic crash and he's just at the edge. We teach employees how to deescalate that and shift them to the right resources and assets and so forth."

"We're {also} training businesses and other entities . . . how to recognize something that is out of place or that makes no sense," he continued. "You see a guy walking in a full-length winter coat and it's ninety degrees outside, there is an issue with that. Some people are just so hesitant to call the police, well they don't want people to be mad at them or they don't want to seem like they're racists in this day and age; you have to get over all that stuff. The public is becoming more and more sensitive, because of the current situation, with what's going on out there. I think we catch more burglars than we ever have. People are paying attention, looking for everything. Everything else, be it technology from an alarm with good video, video that doesn't erase over itself in six hours or eight hours, and just the vigilance of all involved."

Training material should cover robbery prevention and appropriate response procedures. This includes how to quickly get a mental description of the criminal to pass along to the police. There should also be an emphasis put on cooperating with robbers without fear of repercussions. Employees should never put themselves in harm's way to try to save the business' money. Also, all employees should be made aware of installed security systems, but only key personnel trained on how to properly operate these systems.

The Bottom Line

Remember all the locks and alarm systems you install only work when they're used properly. Any business security measures you implement won't matter without sufficient employee training and protocols in place. Be sure you establish a routine with closing staff to ensure doors and windows are suitably locked, all monies are deposited or appropriately locked safely away in the safe and alarm systems set nightly.

As the rising cost of crime escalates and further cuts into small businesses' profits, it's vital that business owners increase preventative measures and continue to develop innovative methods of crime detection and deterrence. Without making these critical advances, your business could become unprofitable and susceptible to closure.

CHAPTER 5

||||||||||||||||||||||||||||||||||||||||||||||

Crime Monitoring and Integrated Technology

Changes in technology affect both those seeking to better protect themselves and their property and the criminals who strive to find easier, less vulnerable ways to break the law. The difference is how each side incorporates new technologies and how quickly it's implemented. Upgrading to new security systems is often a slow process, especially on a city-wide level. Implementation by the community as a whole requires the ability to agree on the best tools and/or tactics and coordinate these efforts, and, in city-wide endeavors, a lengthy bureaucratic procurement process is often the norm.

Meanwhile, criminals are frequently more adaptable and adopt new technologies immediately to stay ahead of law enforcement's efforts to crack down on crime. Furthermore, criminals only need to find one flaw in a security plan, which may allow them to infiltrate even the most advanced networks. Alternately, whether it's from an individual or a city-wide safety protection standpoint, law abiding and law enforcing community members have to defend against every possible plan of attack imaginable. Following each unique form of attack, technology responds with new, better ways to thwart efforts to utilize this same avenue in future attacks.

Cities tend to be reactive in security, but to even the playing field and create safer cities, communities must learn to use technological advances to prevent crime in a more proactive manner. Some technology only benefits those in defensive roles against crime, such as fingerprint technology and advanced residential and business alarm systems. Everyone should use these types of resources to the fullest advantage, since criminals typically can't use them to their advantage. You should also research and seriously consider a wealth of other high-tech wizardry that aid in crime monitoring and integration. This should include city-wide surveillance systems that incorporate updated camera and audio feeds with digital capabilities, and vital acoustic and optical sensors, such as thermal imaging and gunshot detection technology.

Cameras and Audio Feeds

Cameras play a huge role in surveillance and camera technology has come a long way since the grainy images seen from small black and white monitors and VCR recordings. Digital infrastructures, network convergence, wireless connectivity and even cloud services have prompted great strides in cameras with not only video, but also audio, surveillance capabilities.

Surveillance cameras with audio feeds combined with sophisticated software packages are swiftly becoming necessary components in reducing crime, augmenting law enforcement's capabilities and keeping a city safe. These systems are recognized as one of the most effective tools police departments can implement, and despite potential budget constraints, city-wide video surveillance is becoming more cost-effective, valuable and realistic for any size city throughout the country.

There are many benefits to citywide video/audio surveillance, but one of the most important is the addition of more eyes and ears on the streets. Trained staff can actually track suspects, identify them via facial recognition software, listen to what's going on and sometimes even issue verbal commands until patrol units arrive. Video/audio surveillance aids in verifying criminal activity or dangerous situations, so police officers can be dispatched quickly to intervene in active scenarios. This not only provides important data that tells police officers what they're walking into, which helps keep them safe, but it also gets them where they need to be faster, which can greatly reduce crime throughout the city. This improves citizen and business safety, which can also lead to stronger, better community relations. These systems also provide the foundation for ancillary sensors that can enhance the video and/or audio feeds, such as thermal imaging and gunshot detection.

Plus, these systems don't stop at real-time assistance, they're also set up to capture and document events. So, rather than relying on eyewitness statements that often vary from person to person, cities can record and conclusively discern what happened in any given situation. Recording a vast amount of footage, however, usually requires cities to procure and maintain large servers that could eat away at a limited budget. Instead, they might consider utilizing secure cloud technology where they can extend video retention periods and ensure availability of video archives. They can also choose to partially use their own existing server-based systems combined with implementing a cloud service to expand their surveillance efforts.

When choosing specific cameras, there are several factors city officials should consider. For example, the field of view and movement of a specific camera can greatly affect how many cameras are needed and the placement of these cameras. Field of view simply refers to how wide of an area the camera can see and record; the greater viewing field, the less cameras required, which saves money. Also, a camera that can pan and/or tilt is almost mandatory for full functionality in citywide security efforts. This is just because a stationary or static camera won't be able to cover nearly as large an area, but also because it hampers the ability for trained staff members to track specific subjects as they leave the scene of a crime.

It's also critical to choose cameras with high resolution. A camera with a low resolution can greatly affect the quality of the video and sometimes even render it useless. Cameras with a resolution high enough to supply clearly visible images to more easily identify faces and/or objects in real-time and for recordings are a must-have quality in the equipment you choose. This is also where thermal imaging can partially come into play, with night vision capabilities that allow cameras to see and record images in little or no light situations. This could have the greatest impact on the effectiveness of a city's system, because, historically, more criminal activity tends to occur at night. I'll discuss the overall importance of thermal imaging in the next section.

Finally, the audio features a specific camera provides is also vital in both receiving and potentially emitting sound. A camera's audio features could include a microphone, speaker or both depending on a city's specific needs. Cameras with both are more useful because they can double as an intercom. This can become a highly important feature when you need to issue voice commands until patrol units can arrive at the scene.

Besides the feeds from city government-owned cameras, it's important for police and city personnel to form partnerships with businesses and other organizations who have their own surveillance systems. This allows even better coverage of the city by linking to and utilizing video and/or audio feeds from already established systems. Cities must a system that's flexible and scalable if they wish to continue expanding their security efforts and want the system to combine well with current and future video analytics.

Thermal Imaging

Installing sensors on city-owned cameras mounted around the municipality can bring a wealth of other data and/or early warning signals. One such sensor performs thermal imaging detection. This is invaluable to police departments for viewing images over great distances at any light level. It's also ideal for fire departments in detecting live fires and identify hot spots to prevent fires before they occur.

As previously mentioned, thermal imaging encompasses night vision technologies. It's a method of improving the visibility of objects located in dark environments by detecting their infrared radiation, then creating an image based on this information. Besides thermal imaging, a city's night vision endeavors might alternately include low-light imaging or near-infrared illumination. Unlike these two alternatives, thermal imaging doesn't require ambient light, which makes it the better choice. Thermal imaging can also penetrate through haze, smoke and fog. While near-infrared illumination also has this capability, low-light imaging does not.

Thermal imaging can be a highly useful law enforcement tool, because it can provide sharp images in total darkness and any weather conditions. By utilizing thermal imaging in a citywide surveillance system, you take away visibility challenges from weather to environmental issues, which better ensures that any risk to a city's safety, security and stability is clearly spotted and an appropriate response is made sooner. Strategically placed thermal imaging sensors provide law enforcement with a tactical advantage that could very well change the outcome of a dangerous situation.

Law enforcement personnel also benefit from handheld, portable thermal imaging cameras at night or during poor weather conditions. These smaller devices carried by police officers also offer much-needed thermal imaging capabilities, but in a much more compact solution. These devices allow them to see farther than regular binoculars and pick up the heat signatures from even the smallest sources, such as the breath of a suspect hiding behind an object, trying to avoid detection or running down a dark alley, trying to flee the scene. Citizens throughout the world were able to see thermal imaging capabilities in action in April 2013 when law enforcement used this technology to locate one of the Boston Marathon bombing suspects who was hiding inside a tarp-covered boat.

Thermal imaging also provides immediate, critical information in a variety of situations where police officers require eyes in complete darkness or difficult environmental conditions. Thermal imaging is a complete game changer between an officer walking into a dark alley unprepared for what awaits or having the ability to walk into the area knowing what lies ahead. It could mean the difference between life and death in some situations.

Fire departments benefit from this technology in a different, but invaluable way, as well. Thermal imaging cameras embedded with fire detection features and fire risk software with algorithms available not only can detect existing fires, but also probable fires. These systems literally see heat, which can make them indispensable in preventing fires, especially possible forest fires. To get the maximum benefit from this technology, a city's system should include both types of algorithms, one that detects active fires and one that detects fire risks.

With this technology in place, cities can detect a wild fire within two to 10 seconds, depending on the application. Quicker alerts about active fires help protect the community from being devastated by a fire already burning out of control before a call is ever made to the fire department. Even better, is the system's capability of detecting fire risks or hot spots. This algorithm works with the thermal optic's ability to see heat levels and allows it to alert fire responders when a given area exceeds a specified heat threshold, indicating it could catch on fire. This could be invaluable in forests where fire responders could receive earlier alerts and are able to neutralize smoldering wood before it becomes a full-blown wildfire that destroys acres of forest land. It can also be beneficial in urban areas where a fire started in the interior of a building might not be noticed until the building is engulfed in flames that are visible from the outside.

Besides surveillance and crime fighting, thermal imaging also provides assistance in protecting infrastructure like pipelines and power plants, search and rescue operations and more. With all the various benefits found in thermal imaging capabilities, it's clear the important role it plays in keeping cities safer. Many larger cities have already implemented some form of thermal optics in their security plans, but any city can benefit from upgrading old systems or installing new systems that utilize this technology.

Gunshot Detection Technology

Another valuable sensor for citywide surveillance systems is gunshot detection technology. For law enforcement, gunshot detectors let them know when a weapon has been discharged. While this technology was first deployed in an urban setting in the 90s, its widespread use and acceptance only began over the last decade. To realize the worth of these systems and learn how an investment in this technology benefits the community, it's fundamental for city officials to understand how these systems work, how accurate they are and the actual impact they have on police response time.

Within seconds of a shot being fired, a gunshot detection system uses acoustic sensing technology to differentiate sounds as being gunfire, then reports any identified gunshot. When the sensors actually detect the sound of a gun being fired, the system sends a message to police dispatchers, who then decide whether officers should be sent to the scene. Unfortunately, gunshot detection systems can't detect shots being fired indoors or those blocked by buildings or other obstructions, which raises the question of their actual value.

In answer to this question, researchers at the University of Cincinnati performed a study sponsored by the National Institute of Justice (NIJ) to compare various systems in different scenarios with different weapons. They found in most cases, these systems had about an 80% detection accuracy in field tests using blank rounds, which are harder to detect than live ammunition. Systems that use algorithms to triangulate the location of gunfire were capable of pinpointing the exact location of a gunshot within a 25-foot margin of error 72% of the time. While the study didn't find a decrease in response time from citizen reported gunfire when compared to technology-generated reports, there were more reports generated from gunshot detection technology than from citizens. This is partially due to false reporting by the system, but was also largely due to the high rate of unreported gunfire in the area used in the study.

While the study's design and the relatively early stage of development for this technology could have hampered the results, there are many potentially valuable uses for these systems. For example, detecting previously unreported gunfire could have significant ramifications for future crime analysis and prevention of criminal activity in cities seeking to control random gunfire issues. While this use may only benefit some cities, gunshot detection systems can also serve as rapid response tools and valuable crime prevention tools. They can also act as a deterrent should police want to publicize the use of the system and the fact that it would increase the likelihood of apprehending people who fire weapons either during the commission of a crime or randomly discharging a gun for no apparent reason. The initial research of these systems was very promising and with the evolution of gunshot detection technology, the accuracy and portability issues are being resolved.

These highly effective tools are now being deployed in municipal police departments throughout the country. Typically, these systems use a mesh of wirelessly-connected acoustic sensors that the cities attach to light poles and roof tops. When properly installed, these sensors more consistently alert police dispatch of gunfire much more rapidly than civilian reports. Plus, GPS (global positioning system) capabilities help these sensors pinpoint the exact location of any shots fired. The data collected from these sensors also allow police departments to analyze gun-related activity trends and track gunfire in any given area. Sensors also record every gunshot detected, which can help distinguish the caliber of the weapon fired and even the exact position of where it was fired and when.

These systems have the potential to increase the efficiency of a police force, while also providing added tools for investigations. This makes the technology a definite advantage in fighting crime, however, some law enforcement personnel still worry over the accuracy of these systems. To combat this, vendors are working with police to help mitigate false alerts by keeping the systems adjusted or calibrated to be more accurate. They're also offering remote monitoring services to verify whether a sound is an actual gunshot or other disturbance, such as a vehicle backfire or fireworks. The monitoring company performs this analysis in seconds and sends an alert to local police should the sound be confirmed as actual gunfire. This often delivers a substantial reduction in false alerts, which makes it a more reliable tool.

As these systems become stronger and more reliable, an investment in the technology makes sense. Although some law enforcement agencies have offset the cost through federal grants, investing in these systems are often met with budget constraints. Despite financial and potential privacy issues, many citizens find these systems to be a comforting reassurance. They feel that even when the police can't be physically present, the neighborhood's safety is being watched over, so implementation of this technology continues to grow.

These technological advances are just part of the many ways a city increases its security and safety. There are many other tools available that assist in the detection of crime and apprehension of criminals. Cities can further enhance their efforts with advanced high-definition license plate recognition readers, face and voice recognition software and radioactive material detection sensors, just to name a few valuable technological advances.

Many of these security tools don't just augment law enforcement's capabilities, they also assist fire departments, traffic management, emergency management and other public safety offices. Advanced technology that continuously monitors a city gives appropriate personnel a head start on dealing with emergency situations and allows them to potentially prevent some threatening events from occurring. These are definite perks of investing in citywide crime monitoring and integrated technology.

How has technology changed surveillance?

Technology has radically changed the way we protect our homes, businesses, and communities. On a local, state and national level, technology has also definitely changed surveillance techniques. As these changes make citizens safer, there is a long-standing conflict between protecting people's lives and protecting their privacy. While enhanced technology helps improve surveillance, it not only makes security more proactive but in some people's opinion, more intrusive to their privacy. First, let's consider how technology has changed surveillance and other security measures for the better.

In our homes and businesses, the digital age has brought what used to be only possible in science fiction to a gradual reality. This includes smart systems you can monitor while you're away. It also includes remote monitoring systems that allow you to view your home and/or business from anywhere with cellphone and/or Internet service. You can now stream real-time video and audio directly to your smartphone or tablet and save these feeds to review later, if necessary. The shift in technology gives home and business owners surveillance possibilities never dreamed of just a few short years ago.

In the community, city-wide surveillance systems can utilize the same kinds of technology deployed to catch terrorist. These systems watch over an entire city to identify everything from the largest threats to the most mundane activities like preventing vandalism. Surveillance systems rapidly increase in value when software and other technologies are added to support law enforcement's desire to keep cities safe. This includes software that can automatically mine your surveillance footage to find specific information, such as faces, voices, license plates or other specified objects in a massive, searchable database.

One prime example of the advancements in surveillance technology is when authorities sifted through a monumental amount of footage gathered from government and private surveillance cameras and even shots from smartphones taken by bystanders following the Boston Marathon bombing in April 2013. It took the FBI only three days to secure shots (found on a department store's camera) of the two suspects, that despite being blurry, were identifiable. While this may seem like too long, compare this turnaround time to the London bombings in 2005, in which it took 1,000s of investigators weeks to sort through and interpret the city's closed-circuit television footage following these attacks.

Not only has surveillance camera technology changed, but also the software and algorithms that enhance this technology, have all come a long way in just those eight years, and the technology continues to evolve daily. A prime example is the September 2016 NJ/NY bombings when the suspected bomber was quickly identified on one of more than 8,000 (government and privately owned) surveillance cameras that New York has added since the 9/11 attacks.

Camera installation in NY has steadily increased over the last 15 years and so has the use of more sophisticated surveillance technology in the New York Police Department's (NYPD) efforts to monitor the city and fight crime. Now, NY's real-time camera feeds can be found throughout the city, including in its bridges and tunnels, subways and main train and bus stations.

These feeds are monitored by NYPD watch officers at the Lower Manhattan Security Coordination Center where they also keep tabs on gunshot detection, radiation and biological and chemical sensors. These officers, along with analysts, monitor alerts on suspicious persons or activities utilizing advanced video analytics. These analytics use information gleaned from face, license plate and object-detection technology that also helps them to track people, vehicles and even unattended packages.

Data from all the city's linked cameras and detectors, license plate readers, 9-1-1 calls and crime databases are fed into their map-based Domain Awareness System (DAS). This system analyzes all the information and correlates it with potential threats. While the NYPD began using advanced video analytic software on selected feeds in 2010, this more complete analytics system was launched in 2012 and regularly adds even more sources of data to its network on a regular basis.

These surveillance and security measures aren't surprising in a city with a history of violence, including the first World Trade

Center bombing back in 1993. Other cities try to emulate NY's efforts, although usually on a smaller scale, with the intention of protecting their cities in the same capacity. In major cities particularly, the age of terrorism means someone is almost always watching for anything construed as suspicious in nature. Though built on a smaller scale, Boston's camera network also proved the undeniable power of surveillance systems, their ability to help solve crimes, and, hopefully, prevent similar incidents from occurring in the future.

These local technologies may also be utilized on a nationwide level, but with even more sophisticated surveillance capabilities added to the mix. Currently, the U.S. faces very real, serious national security threats. Terrorism continues to flourish worldwide and the U.S. isn't immune to these threats, as seen in previous terrorist attacks made upon the country. To combat these threats, national and military leaders, policy makers and law enforcement need to understand who the country's adversaries are, where they're at, what they're capable of and what kinds of plans and intentions do they have. It's the job of the National Security Agency (NSA) and Central Security Service (CSS) to provide this information. The U.S. Department of Homeland Security (DHS) also helps monitor threats to help enhance the Nation's security.

NSA/CSS provides relevant foreign intelligence through surveillance of communications and information systems in its Signals Intelligence (SIGINT) program. This information is used to protect America's troops, support its allies, combat international crime and narcotics, fight terrorism and other important objectives. DHS, on the other hand, closely monitors domestic attacks on public places and gatherings to further enhance national security on a continual basis. DHS engages with community and private sector partners to provide recommendations about protective measures they should implement. It also provides tools and resources, free of charge, to communities, because these communities are the first line of defense in maintaining public safety and security.

Besides both of these department's efforts, the Central Intelligence Agency's (CIA) In-Q-Tel identifies, adapts and delivers innovative technology solutions by finding and funding promising security-related technology. This includes investing in promising ventures, such as more advanced face and object recognition software that not only recognizes faces but goes even deeper by detecting a person's approximate age, gender, and other demographic information, and even their mood. The information gleaned from these programs is stored in databases that can uncover much-needed clues in a simple, 15-second search query.

While all these improvements in surveillance technology helps keep everyone on a local, state and national level safer, there will always remain privacy concerns from a number of citizens, and even more frequently from civil-liberties activists. These concerns are most often about how surveillance technology could be abused in a variety of ways. However, there are others who feel the benefits of surveillance technology far outweigh any fears a person might have about privacy. For example, when compared to other security measures, surveillance cameras are frequently the less costly, more effective choice.

They can also be less intrusive in certain situations, as pointed out by Farhad Manjoo, an American journalist and technology columnist who previously wrote for *The Wall Street* and now writes for *The New York Times.* He mentioned that when combined with competent law enforcement, surveillance cameras are a much more pleasant alternative to being subjected to pat-downs and metal detectors like those used in airports, concerts and other public venues and celebrations. He makes a good point.

Following the 9/11 attacks, there may be situations where security should trump privacy in order to keep the public safe. This brings us back to citizen concerns that while surveillance cameras make many people feel more secure knowing the "bad guys" are being watched, others, including privacy advocates, are uneasy about the idea that "good guys" are being monitored, as well. The whole apprehension over "Big Brother" is watching you, could hamper the installation of valuable safety and security measures in the future. Compromises between security and privacy will need to be made to ensure public safety is upheld both nationally and on a local level. Because, maintaining a safe city is increasingly more challenging for local municipalities and law enforcement agencies, and they can do it much more effectively with community involvement.

As the crime rates increase, the demand for appropriate security measures has a hard time keeping pace, especially when combined with budgetary issues. Cities can often enhance their security measures by pooling resources, and making sure any technologies they add are scalable and sustainable when dealing with limited funds. Again, the community can help these efforts by taking part in watch programs and linking private security systems in businesses and other organizations with a city-wide network.

The potential value of public surveillance technology always takes on new meaning when suspects are identified and even caught using this technology, but going forward almost always comes down to cost. However, many cities have found that the cost savings associated with averting crime paid for the systems they installed. Home and business owners can look at it the same way. Even if you only avoid one property crime and your family and belongings are kept safe from this one incident, then the system has paid for itself.

However, even after Boston identified bombing suspects through security-camera images, some city officials say blanketing a city in surveillance cameras could create as many problems as it solves. While a broad network of surveillance cameras scattered along city streets and public spaces increases the likelihood of catching criminals on video, the amount of evidence generated can be overwhelming without the proper software, algorithms and training to use the systems correctly, which means looking for further funding and personnel capable of dealing with these systems. Again, federal grants often help offset these expenditures.

Many cities found that the most effective systems contained enough cameras to detect crimes in progress and were monitored by trained staff. These systems included technology integrated into all areas of law enforcement activities. Remember it takes a community effort to keep cities safe, so these systems also require help from private sectors working with police to fully connect every area of the city.

City-wide safety and security means protecting the public from threats, both foreign and domestic. Technological advances will continue to enhance the ability to successfully monitor the entire city, and by extension, this technology will further aid law enforcement efforts to prevent crime and catch criminals. Through a concerted effort from the highest government officials to ordinary citizens, everyone should be dedicated to making cities safer. This includes protecting people from natural and man-made disasters and all types of crimes in the real world and cyber-crimes in the cyber world. In the coming years, there's no question that cities will become "smarter" and more connected in ways possibly not even imaginable today, and the technology that brings it all together will keep cities safe now and for many generations to come.

EPILOGUE

||||||||||||||||||||||||||||||||||||

After reading my book, I'm sure you realize the overall importance of community safety and the value of collaborative efforts to reach security goals. The techniques and tools discussed in this book are just some of the available resources to decrease crime and increase safety throughout a city. Hopefully, it also increased your awareness of the obstacles many city's face in various safety endeavors. With your behind-the-scenes look, you've probably realized there's so much more that goes on than you ever imagined.

Whether you're dealing with large community gatherings or day-to-day community life, as you've read, city officials and emergency responders face numerous challenges trying to ensure the physical safety of all citizens. Along with traditional crime, a wide spectrum of potential threats including man-made tragedies, natural disasters, terrorist attacks (both foreign and domestic) and other catastrophic events, all jeopardize the safety and security of a city and have an immediate impact on the quality of life of its citizens. Behind-the-scenes efforts, collaborative efforts between law enforcement and citizens enhance cities' security measures and it's important to understand how everyone does their part.

Any city's safety efforts begin with individual citizens. Business owners and private citizens concerned about personal safety must become proactive in keeping their city safe. This often means building partnerships with police personnel and actively participating in community policing efforts. Although residents and businesses often have conflicting interests, everyone should strive to work together for the common good -- to build a safer community. Neighbors, whether in a residential or business area, should look out for each other and know and work with police. Together, these are powerful ingredients in community safety and those who take a

leadership role are often linchpins for achieving and sustaining city-wide security. Homeowners can do their part by securing their own residences and starting or assisting with neighborhood watch groups and various community improvement projects. United, formalized neighborhood groups not only help eliminate longstanding criminal activities and deep-rooted violence, it also helps deter new crime. Improvement projects doesn't just make the community look more beautiful, many of these projects also deter illegal activities.

Business owners can likewise add or upgrade security systems in their buildings and learn more about linking or integrating their system's audio and/or video feeds to a centralized, law enforcement surveillance system. This further enhances police personnel's crime monitoring efforts, which benefits the entire city. Taking part in revitalization programs and community improvement projects also help businesses deter crime.

Anyone with a security system should also take appropriate steps to ensure those accessing the system knows how to properly use it, to avoid taking police officers off more vital calls to answer a false alarm. Everyone in the community should make a concentrated effort to get to know local law enforcement and learn more about partnering with them for a safer community overall. Private citizens and business owners engaged in helping identify possible criminal activities, terrorist threats and infrastructure vulnerabilities are doing their part in keeping the city safe.

On the law enforcement front, local police and sheriffs' departments have powerful resources to combat crime, but they still cannot make the community safer by themselves -- it requires a community effort. It's recognized that community policing movements aren't successful without citizen participation. Police departments commit to community policing to proactively solve the concerns and problems within specific neighborhoods and are increasingly willing to work with local businesses, organizations, community developers, city agencies, nonprofits, other service providers and residents to tackle crime and the root causes of illegal activities using every resource available. This united front also helps promote stronger problem-solving solutions that might even help eliminate hot spots of illegal activity that may not have relented with prior crime control efforts.

Throughout their duties, many law enforcement efforts take place outside the public eye, but always in an effort to protect and serve every citizen to the fullest potential. Emergency response personnel and city governments alike often do their part in keeping the city safe while also fighting budget constraints. Although, you should now have a better understanding of these behind-the-scenes activities, for more information, consider attending a public safety open house or citizen police academy. These programs teach you even more about all their various activities and allow further interaction with police and other emergency personnel.

Numerous city and county agencies and officials are also essential in city-wide efforts to reduce crime. Besides those that support emergency response activities, departments with resources in economic development, code enforcement and sanitation can be particularly helpful. These offices help ensure that city development projects and code enforcement operations, as well as, other organizing efforts yield results on a collaborative scale that not only reduce crime, but also promote community cohesion.

The myriad of efforts from all these different groups of people aren't to just displace criminal activity from one location to another, where it'll just begin again. If the illegal activity can't be stopped completely, then the hope is to diffuse it, so it's thinly spread out over a large area, instead of concentrated in a small one where it's easier to control and operate their illegal business ventures. This is where technology joins the behind-the-scenes efforts to monitor these activities throughout the city when staffing issues limit police efforts to be everywhere at once.

From a technology standpoint, previous security efforts should evolve with technological advances to further enhance public safety city-wide. Because, in the end, safe cities are smart cities. This isn't only through critical human collaborations, but also embracing the advances in technology that make security efforts even easier. Using technology can increase the effectiveness of traditional crime-fighting techniques by integrating effective security solutions through next generation technology. This isn't just convenient, but necessary, especially in crime-riddled urban locales. These solutions more efficiently address crime detection and prevention, while also helping to gather intelligence and share all this vital information between essential government offices and emergency response departments. This makes compatible, collaborative security solutions invaluable in effectively combining every department's resources in a mass attempt to keep the city safe.

Technologies, such as surveillance cameras and analytic and mapping programs shouldn't be implemented in an isolated area, but undertaken as part of a comprehensive, city-wide endeavor. When you have the tools and technology needed to more adequately fight and prevent crime and respond quicker and more efficiently to potential threats, it not only promotes a safer environment for the masses, it promotes a sense of safety and well-being among citizens. A collaborative sharing of information between citizens and police in a community-police partnership helps alleviate fears of invasions of privacy, while also providing additional community development and safety initiatives that combine with traditional policing and technology innovations.

Public safety is everyone's concern. Cities must approach crime prevention in smart, collaborative and effective ways. Dispelling the firm grip of fear on a community can be accomplished when you combine good urban design, sound safety procedures and practices, cooperative security endeavors and modern, security-minded technology. Safe streets are critical to build sustainable communities and every community member does their part to curb crime one street, then one block at a time, until the entire city is a safer place for everyone.

ABOUT THE AUTHOR

||||||||||||||||||||||||||||||||||||||||||||||||||||||||||||||||||||||||||||||||

Robert Hessel is the founder and CEO of Source 1 Solutions an IT Services organization recognized for providing commercial security systems to enterprise clients. At any given time his company is responsible for helping protect over 100 billion dollars worth of assets for clients like: The Dali Museum, Amalie Arena, The Florida Aquarium, and the US Airforce. He is an expert contributor on the Real Estate Radio Quarterback Show and Tampa Bay Magazine and has been featured on the cover of Security Dealer Magazine. In 2014 his company was named Honeywell Commercial Security Dealer of the year for North America. Robert is also a Veteran of the United States Navy.

Morgan James
Speakers Group

We connect Morgan James published authors with live and online events and audiences who will benefit from their expertise.